D0617804

WHEN MOURNING COMES

WHEN MOURNING COMES

A Book of Comfort for the Grieving

William B. Silverman

and

Kenneth M. Cinnamon

JASON ARONSON INC.
Northvale, New Jersey
London

5·2·22

The authors gratefully acknowledge permission to use the following:

"A Parable of Birth" from THE JEWISH WAY IN DEATH AND MOURNING by
Maurice Lamm (New York: Jonathan David Publishers). Copyright © 1969 by Maurice
Lamm. Reprinted by permission of the author.

Copyright © 1990, 1982 by William B. Silverman

10 9 8 7 6 5 4 3 2 1

All rights reserved. Printed in the United States of America. No part of this book may
be used or reproduced in any manner whatsoever without written permission from
Jason Aronson Inc. except in the case of brief quotations in reviews for inclusion in a
magazine, newspaper, or broadcast.

First softcover edition – 1994

Library of Congress Cataloging-in-Publication Data

Silverman, William B.
    When mourning comes : a book of comfort for the grieving / William B.
Silverman and Kenneth M. Cinnamon.
        p. cm.
    ISBN 0-87668-820-2 (hb) (previously ISBN 0-882229-623-X)
    ISBN 1-56821-184-8 (pb)
    1. Bereavement – Psychological aspects. 2. Death – Psychological
aspects. 3. Grief. 4. Consolation. I. Cinnamon, Kenneth M.
II. Title.
BF575.G7S54 1990
155.9'37 – dc20   89-17771

Manufactured in the United States of America. Jason Aronson Inc. offers books and
cassettes. For information and catalog write to Jason Aronson Inc., 230 Livingston
Street, Northvale, New Jersey 07647.

To Betty

Without whom this book would never have become a reality. She typed the manuscript and gave the book its title. In times of discouragement and despair, she inspired me to persist. Her loving and caring spirit touched every page. It is my hope that the comfort she has given me may reach out in response to the silent scream of those who suffer the anguish of bereavement.

William B. Silverman

I am standing on the seashore. A ship at my side spreads her white sails to the morning breeze and starts for the blue ocean. She is an object of beauty and strength, and I stand and watch her until at length she is only a ribbon of white cloud just where the sea and sky come to join each other. Then someone at my side says: "There! She's gone!" Gone where? Gone from my sight—that is all. She is just as large in mast and hull and spar as she was when she left my side and just as able to bear her load of living freight to their destination. Her diminished size is in me, not in her, for just at the moment when someone at my side says, "There! She's gone!" there are other voices ready to take up the glad shout, "There! She comes!" And that is dying.

—attributed to Col. David "Mickey" Marcus
(1902–1948)

Contents

Introduction

Death is not extinguishing the light;
it is putting out the lamp because the
dawn has come.
> —Rabindranath Tagore

WHEN MOURNING COMES is not about grief. It is a book for the grieving, a book written for you with a pen dipped in tears.

A friend who had recently lost his wife said, "For crying out loud, I wish everyone would leave me alone to suffer in silence." He had never cried; there were no tears. He had shut out the world and was slowly dying inside. He didn't know that grief must be expressed, and that there *is* a time for crying out loud.

After our bitter questions, our protests, our anger, and yes, even our depression, we must finally find ways to work through our grief, one step at a time. And we don't have to do this alone. There are those who can support and strengthen us, but we have to allow them to break through the shell that insulates us from the intrusion of reality. We must learn to respond to others, to touch the hands and the hearts that are reaching out to us.

I Feel So Helpless and So Hopeless

Do you feel that nothing can help in this time of grief? Do you feel that there are no alternatives to suffering?

Think again, because there is something *you* can do! You are not a helpless leaf that is driven by every breeze and wisp of wind. You are not a robot with tears. You are not a puppet manipulated by the strings of circumstance. You are not a human computer programmed for pain.

You are a human being with the will and the power to choose, to say yes or no, and to make a decision to deal with your grief. You can turn your frustration into fulfillment, and transform your tears into a triumph of the human spirit.

That is why this book was written. It was written to help the grieving to convert their sorrow into something sublime. That is why this parable was written for you, for me, and for everyone who has ever cried out from the depths of bereavement:

The Scratch on the Diamond

A king once owned a large, beautiful, pure diamond of which he was justly proud, for it had no equal anywhere. One day, the diamond accidentally sustained a deep scratch. The king called in the most skilled diamond cutters and offered them a great reward if they would remove the imperfection from his treasured jewel. But none could repair the blemish. The king was sorely distressed.

After a time a gifted lapidary came to the king and promised to make the rare diamond even more beautiful than it had been before. The king was impressed by his confidence and entrusted his precious stone to the lapidary's care. And the man kept his word.

With superb artistry he engraved a lovely rosebud around the imperfection. He had used the scratch to make the stem of the flower.

This parable says something to us—it tells us that we have the power to emulate that craftsman. When life bruises and wounds us, when our souls are torn and lacerated with grief, when our hearts are scratched with sorrow, we can use the scratches to etch a portrait of beauty. Out of the sorrow and the anguish can arise something indescribably meaningful.

This can be. This can happen if you determine to make it happen. Only you can make it happen.

You may be thinking, "Do you believe for one moment that I want to feel dead inside myself? Do you think I don't want to respond to those who are so near and dear to me? Do you think I want to be so hopeless and so helpless? I don't! I've tried to come out of it, but I can't."

The fact is, you can—if you choose to. Reading this far is a sign that you are making a choice. Together we can begin to take the first steps in coming up and out of your grief.

1

With No Language But a Cry

❧ ❧

The only cure for grief is to grieve.
—Joshua Loth Liebman

Y OU ARE HURTING. There is an aching emptiness
that cries within. There are no words. There is no
sound. There is only silent screaming.

While thoughts collide in mindless confusion you are
still able to protest, question, and demand to know:
"Why me? Why did it have to happen to someone so
good, someone I loved and who loved me? There is no
reason for this. The whole thing doesn't make any
sense."

Some of your friends may have told you that it is
selfish to ask "Why me?" at a time of grief. Do not listen
to them. You have a right to say, "I hurt. I am brokenhearted and lost. I experience it. I feel it, so I have a
right to ask 'Why me?' Why isn't the whole world aware .
of my suffering? How many people out there even
care? So even with the best of intentions, do not dis-
count my sorrow. It is my sorrow, and I am not going
to minimize or deny it."

A difficult and painful path lies ahead, but there will be light as you proceed. We understand what Tennyson meant when he wrote at such a time of sorrow, "What am I? An infant crying in the night, an infant crying for the light, and with no language but a cry." But we are not infants. We have cried enough and now we must find another language—the language of hope, of determination, and of action. Where shall we begin?

CONFRONTING SORROW

We begin by facing our grief with all its anguish, despair, fear, and anger. Someone we love is dead. There is nothing we can do to bring that person back to us. Will we accept this, knowing that there is no medicine that can assuage the pain of bereavement, and no surgery that can put together the fragments of a broken heart?

There is no simple way to endure bereavement and the suffering that attends it. All of us will rationally accept the fact that death is inevitable for everyone else. But for ourselves? For those we love? We resist. We fight. We struggle. We want to close our eyes and our minds to the inevitability of death. We cannot understand why there should be the dark night of the soul, but it is there enveloping us in sad embrace, dominating, consuming, and possessing us.

There are times when we think we cannot go on. All the reserves have been depleted. We have to come to the end of ourselves. There seem to be no more tomorrows, no more hope, no light, strength, or reason for living. How we would love to yield to forgetfulness, to close our eyes and just go to sleep. But we cannot and we must not. The words of Robert Frost remind us:

The woods are lovely, dark and deep.
But I have promises to keep,
And miles to go before I sleep,
And miles to go before I sleep.*

What will help us go on? Faith? Memory?

It is difficult to maintain faith or even a quest for living when those who once brought faith to our lives have died and only memory can fill the emptiness their passing leaves behind. Memory can tell us what we were in the company of those we love. Memory can support us and make us feel less alone. Those who live no more echo still within our thoughts, our words, our hearts, and our feelings. Their lives have become woven into what we are. Yet memory alone cannot help us to find what each of us must now become.

When we remember our dear ones who no longer walk in the land of the living and we weep for them, somehow we penetrate the very core of ourselves. We begin to think about the brevity of human life, and feel that we have come to the end of ourselves. It is at this time that we begin to understand our grief. We realize that when we mourn for our dear ones, we also mourn for ourselves. We confront the reality of our own death and we are afraid.

When we experience our loss, we feel more than fear. We also feel anger. Our reactions to bereavement sometimes prompt us to rage against life, to shake our fist at the universe, to protest against God, perhaps even to lose our religious faith. That is what happened

---

* From "Stopping by Woods on a Snowy Evening," from *The Poetry of Robert Frost,* edited by Edward Connery Lathem. Copyright 1923, © 1969 by Holt, Rinehart and Winston. Copyright 1951 by Robert Frost. Reprinted by permission of Holt, Rinehart and Winston, Publishers.

to a young Welsh poet, Dylan Thomas. As his father was dying, he poured out his feelings of outrage and bitterness in one of his most famous poems:

> Do not go gentle into that good night
> Old age should burn and rave at close of day;
> Rage, rage against the dying of the light.
> And you, my father, there on the sad height,
> Curse, bless, me now with your fierce tears, I pray.
> Do not go gentle into that good night.
> Rage, rage against the dying of the light.*

Isn't that what we do? Instead of letting our dear ones go gentle into that good night of peace, instead of allowing their memory to inspire us to beauty, love, and inner calm, we rage against the dying of the light. We identify death with grief, misery, and anguish. We protest against the very nature of the universe. What kind of a tribute is it to our dear ones when we feel that their death has made us lose faith in life, in goodness, in our religion, and even in God? We do not pay tribute to their memory by raging against life or death. But what do we do when there seems to be no answer to our pleas and entreaties for solace?

We must confront our grief. We have been taught, and we in turn teach others, to be ashamed of tears. And so deep emotions are often pushed into the inner recesses of our personalities, and counselors, clergymen, and doctors receive dry-eyed people who are weeping inside. We must look at our grief and refuse to turn away. We must give full expression to our grief and permit the torment to pour from our souls. It is when our hearts are too filled to take any more that sorrow overflows through our eyes.

---

* *The Poems of Dylan Thomas.* Copyright 1952 by Dylan Thomas. Reprinted by permission of New Directions.

GRIEF MUST BE EXPRESSED

The insights of modern psychology make it clear that grief must be expressed or there may be serious consequences. So many people say, "I know it's selfish of me to weep, but . . ." If someone hits you over the head with a baseball bat and tears come to your eyes, no one is going to say, "You're being selfish to cry." No! You've been hurt. So it is with grief. Deep ties of a relationship have been severed. You have been deeply wounded in your loss and you need to cry. Grief is a normal and necessary part of life, and so are tears.

Psychologists speak of grief work—that is, grief as something to be worked through. To do this you must be able to face reality and express emotion. Get it out! It does not help you to deny the reality of death, or to read a poem such as "There Is No Death: He's Only Gone Away" and delude yourself into thinking that nothing has really happened. Something has happened. Life can never be the same. You feel not only a profound sense of loss, but resentment and anger toward the doctor, the clergyman, God, and yes, even anger toward yourself.

Now it is time to think about returning to life and creating new life patterns. As one man said after a prolonged period of bereavement, "Somehow I must find the way to put the stars back into my sky." This is part of our journey through the valley of the shadow of death—to keep going until the time we can put the stars back in the sky and live for our loved ones and for ourselves. To remember the ones we lost with sorrow, yes—to remember them with tears, yes—but also to remember them with joy, laughter, and love.

What will ease the pain of bereavement? Where are the words, the thoughts, and the faith that will fill this vacuum? You cannot force grief to disappear. You cannot will it to fly away, because "grief has no wings." Nor can you run away from it. You must face grief courageously, seeking the strength of faith that will enable you to go on. You must be realistic about life and about death. You must recognize that death is inevitable for everyone and everything that lives. Even though you may protest and cry out against the inevitability of death, deep within your heart you must accept it not only as the law of life, but as the law of the universe.

WHEN WE DIE INSIDE

It is this recognition of the inevitability of death that makes us appreciate all the more our past blessings in life. We must not only memorialize our dead, but we must recognize the nobility and the sanctity of life. And though we may protest bitterly against life, saying, "I wish that I had never been born," or "I wish that I were dead," there is also inside us a will to live that is stronger and more compelling than the yearning for death.

There is something else that you must think about now, and it is one of the most difficult of all losses to work through. That is the grief and the loss that we the living experience when we have died inside.

A young man once said to me after losing his wife, "I really feel dead inside. Do you think I will ever be alive again?" Albert Schweitzer put it this way: "The tragedy of life is what dies inside a person while he lives." If you are to "come alive" again, you cannot do it alone.

A small boy struggled to lift a heavy stone, but he could not budge it. The boy's father stopped to watch his efforts and said to his son, "Are you using all your strength?" "Yes, I am," the boy said with irritation.

"No," the father said calmly, "You're not. You have not asked me to help you."

You cannot do it all yourself. You need the help of your friends and dear ones whom you may have already shut out. You need the help of faith and memory to enable you to look within, to find an untapped source of strength.

Do not be afraid to confront grief. Do not be afraid to express your sense of loss. Do not be afraid or ashamed of your tears. Do not pull down the blinds that shut out light and love. One step at a time, you can return to life and begin to live again so that you may be able to put the stars back into your sky.

One Step at a Time!

Confront your sorrow.

❧ ☙

Express your grief.

❧ ☙

Face your fears and your anger.

❧ ☙

Determine to live again.

❧ ☙

Accept the help of others.

❧ ☙

Make a start to put the stars back into your sky.

2

Why, God, Why?

❧ ❧

Sorrow is like a toothache in your heart.
—Henrich Heine

YOU WANT TO FIND a way out of your grief. You want the emotional agony to stop. You want to start to live again. After asking, "Why me?" there is another question that is commonly asked, and that is, "Why, God, why? Why should one so good be taken from me so soon and so young?"

Do not be afraid to ask it. Do not hold back from emptying the protests and the questions from your innermost being. It is not blasphemous or irreverent. It is a question that trembles on your lips, hovers over your mind, and haunts your soul.

If God is good, just, and merciful, why did this have to be? You wait for an answer but seem to hear only the frustrating echo of your own questioning voice. You have a right to question. You have a right to protest.

It is understandable that at the time of your loss you should wonder about God, blame God, and sometimes

9

doubt whether there is a God. There is so much confusion and doubt. Where is God's justice in all of this? How can you even associate love and compassion with God when He allows someone you love to die?

Humankind has been asking that same question ever since the dawn of recorded history. Is there an answer? No one has ever offered a completely satisfactory one. We cannot, and we do not think you can either.

We accept in theory the fact that everything that lives must die. In the fall when we look at the multicolored leaves, breathe in the crispness of the autumn air, and witness the clusters of birds in flight, we recognize that all of the living beauty we love is a portent of death—the death of nature. Soon the leaves will fall, the trees will be naked of foliage, the earth will become hard and cold, and the chill will make us shiver. Before too long the ground will be covered with a blanket of snow, and nature will die until spring.

But with the rebirth of life in the spring, field and forest reawaken from the death of winter. Earth and sky resound with the song of life reborn. It will soon be summer, then fall, winter, and spring again. There is an inevitable transition from season to season. We accept this, but we are reluctant to accept the cycle of birth to death in human existence. As soon as a child is born it begins its journey through the seasons of maturation, through the declining years, and then to its ultimate death.

Reason tells us that everything that lives must die. It is part of God's plan for nature. But you and I find it difficult to accept, if not impossible, when it comes to thinking about our own death or the death of those we love. It is always too soon and too young, no matter what the age.

SENSELESS, MEANINGLESS, AND WRONG

I remember when I received a telephone call urging me to get to the hospital right away. A five-year-old child had been hit by a truck and was hovering between life and death.

When I reached the hospital I hurried to the emergency room and found the parents, Linda and Ron, holding each other and sobbing hysterically. The child, Jimmy, was in surgery, and the doctors had not offered much hope.

Ron asked, "Why did this happen? What has he ever done that he should deserve this? Why our child? Why us? It is all so senseless, meaningless, and wrong. Why, God, why?"

When the surgeon came out of the operating room he did not have to tell us—we knew by his face that their son was dead. Linda screamed. Ron put his hands to his head, tearing at his hair, asking, "Why? Why, God, why?"

A few minutes later Ron was saying, "Only a baby. Five years old. What did he do? What was his sin?" And then turning to me in anger he screamed, "You call this a God of love, a God of compassion? Don't you ever mention that to me again. I will never worship that God again as long as I live. I don't want any part of a God who would take away an innocent five-year-old child so young and so soon!" What could I say? What would you have said to the despairing, heartbroken parents?

Later, when I went back to the home to be with Ron and Linda, they both sobbed, "Jimmy was too young. He wasn't ready to die. It's too soon. He was only a child, a little boy. What use could God find for our baby? Why did God do this to us? Why did God do this to Jimmy? Give us an answer, any answer. Show us if there is any sense or meaning to Jimmy's death!"

There was a knock on the door, and a man about sixty years old came into the room. He approached Linda and Ron and said, "I am the truck driver who killed your boy. I don't know what to say." Linda and Ron just looked at him.

The man, crushed by sorrow, spoke falteringly. "I have a grandchild his age. I love children. Even though I wasn't driving fast and it was an accident, I blame myself. Please try to forgive me!"

I then witnessed something so beautiful and compassionate that it remains indelibly imprinted upon my memory.

Linda walked up to the man and put her arms around him as he was sobbing. They both cried, trying to comfort each other. Then Linda said to him, "Don't blame yourself. It wasn't your fault. Please don't blame yourself." She turned away from him and quietly wept.

After protesting and questioning, the young couple faced their grief. It took time, but step by step they worked their way through their sorrow to restructure their lives and live again. They had to. Linda became pregnant again. The future was emerging within her.

GRIEF IS AGELESS

Our hearts go out to those who suffer the loss of a child, but the loss of an adult we love is no less agonizing. It is always too soon for those we love to leave us.

We can understand what Eli Wiesel, the Holocaust survivor and mystic teller of tales, meant when he wrote in his sorrow:

We love You, God, we fear You, we cling to You in spite of You. . . . Forgive me for telling You that You are cheating. You give us reason, but You are its limit and its mirror. You order us to love, but You give that love the taste of ashes. You bless us, and You take back Your blessing. Why are You doing this, to prove what? What truth do You wish to teach us about whom?

When older people die, friends may attempt to comfort us by reminding us of the years they lived and the pain they were spared. This kind of comfort does not help; it just makes us angry and more depressed.

The death of a woman 104 years old taught me the futility of trying to comfort by chronology or longevity. When I went to her daughter's home to make arrangements for the funeral and try to bring her some comfort, the daughter met me with anger and sorrow as she demanded to know, "Tell me, why did God take my mother so young?"

At first I was shocked and amazed that she could even ask that, knowing that her mother had lived to be 104 years old. Then I realized that when you love someone, no matter what the age, that person is always too young to be taken away.

Before I left the house the daughter, who was in her eighties, said, "Someday, maybe someone will be able to answer my questions: 'Why does anyone have to die? If God is so wise and so merciful, why didn't He create a world without pain, suffering, and death?' " These are eternal questions, always in search of an answer.

Age makes little difference in coping with death; death at any age necessitates a change of relationships and life direction. As Shalom Levy said in *Kibbutz*

Hulata, "With the death of a husband or wife you lose your present; with the death of a parent the past; and with the death of a child you lose your future."

A TOOTHACHE IN YOUR HEART

When we ask, "Why, God, why?" the pain would be no less even if our question were answered. A lonesome longing would still ache in our heart. Perhaps that is what the poet Heinrich Heine really meant when he wrote of a "toothache in your heart." The shock of losing a dear one of any age is severe. It results in a tremendous emotional earthquake that stuns, seizes, and pounds you, as you desperately search for something to cling to.

Those who have studied grief reactions are almost unanimously agreed that in its emotional character grief includes elements of fear, guilt, anxiety, and depression. Even certain physical symptoms are normal, such as tightness of the throat, shortness of breath, an empty feeling in the abdomen, general tension, and loneliness. There may be a marked tendency to sigh, and to complain about weakness and exhaustion. Some say, "It is almost impossible to climb up a stairway," or "Everything I lift seems so heavy." "The slightest effort makes me feel tired." "I can't walk to the corner without feeling exhausted." Others do not want to eat. "The food tastes like sand." "I have no appetite at all." "I stuff the food down because I have to eat." "My stomach feels hollow." Some may even experience the same physical symptoms shown by the one who died.

In order to survive the emotional crisis, you must mobilize all the elements in your personality that make for stability—your values, your outlook on life, and your faith. You have to face your grief honestly. You must not be afraid of a confrontation with reality.

Perhaps you are thinking, "You're right, but how do I find the will and the strength to do this?" Before you turn to the "how," it is important for you to look realistically at "what is." You must examine and experience all the painful thoughts and feelings you have, so that you can do something about the hurt.

To begin with, grief is usually accompanied by guilt. It does not necessarily have to be deserved guilt. You may blame yourself falsely and condemn yourself without reason.

"If only I had . . ." or "If only I had not . . ." How many times have we heard this in connection with death? We try to fix the blame for the death of a loved one on ourselves. *We* failed. *We* should have done more— something—anything. Some feel that if we blame someone or something the grief will be eased. This is not so.

Sometimes guilt is expressed, and sometimes it is repressed, or pushed down deep into your mind because you do not want to think about it. Nonetheless, guilt is often there, and you must recognize it and look at it before it can be removed. Despite all your efforts, someone you love died, and you blame yourself. "Why wasn't I more understanding?" "Why didn't I do more?" "Why didn't the doctors find out sooner?"

You may occasionally have dreams about the dead. It may even seem that the loved one is right in the room. Your dreams may be filled with hostility, anxiety, fear, or terror. Other times you may think that you are with the dead, so you must have died, too. There may be frightening thoughts that you do not have long to live and that you will soon die. Fear, confusion, apathy, fatigue, guilt, anxiety, depression, and despair—all are feelings that accompany grief.

You are not abnormal when you feel that you exist in a vacuum of nothingness, and that everything is an unreal, crazy dream. You are not alone when you fear that the feelings you now experience will never go away and will be with you forever. You are not strange or peculiar when you feel utterly brokenhearted, helpless, and numb. These reactions are part of the cycle of grief. That is why you may be trying to retreat into a self-imposed ghetto of bereavement, shutting yourself in and locking the gates of grief so that no one else may enter. You may have withdrawn from all forms of communication with family, friends, and neighbors. And you may have cut off all feelings about God, church, or synagogue.

That is why you may have such a fear of loneliness— a loneliness that is sometimes worse than the fear of death itself. That is why you demand privacy and insist on isolating yourself from others. You just want to be left alone to suffer your sorrow in solitude.

"IT'S GOD'S WILL" AND "EVERYTHING'S GOING TO BE ALL RIGHT"

There are two statements that often aggravate the bereaved. They are: "It's God's will," and "Everything's going to be all right." Has anyone said this to you, even with the best and kindest of intentions?

A father whose son died in a fire at a fraternity house told me, "When my son burned to death, I was angry with God, I was angry with the fraternity, I was angry with life. But I was most angry with those who told me it was the will of God. If I believed it was God's will, I would never go to church again, pray again, or even believe in God again."

It is true that some people do find comfort in believing that whatever happens is God's will. It is God's will that mortal beings cannot live forever. It is God's will that nature obeys natural laws, and that when the heart gives out or the organs cease to function, death will ensue. The existence of death is God's will.

But I do not believe that is what is meant when a person says that "it was God's will" that someone—a child, young person, or an adult—was killed in an automobile accident or died of a congenital deformity. I do not believe that it is God's will when men, women, and children are killed in war. I do not believe that it is God's will that people die in tornadoes, earthquakes, or floods. I cannot go along with the belief that God "needs" a child or a young mother or father and causes them to die. Can you?

Those who die in war are not dead because of the will of God, but because of the will of men, governments, and nations. Those who die in a natural catastrophe do not die because God wills them to die, but because of the immutable laws of nature that are part of God's creation.

Most of us also react negatively to the statement, "Everything's going to be all right." How can everything be all right when someone we love has died? How can everything be all right when life can never be the same? How can everything be all right when there is an emptiness in us that can never again be filled?

Even though life will never be the way it was, we are not doomed to eternal sorrow. We have the power and the will to make things better than they are right now. When mourning comes, instead of simply saying, "It's God's will" or "Everything's going to be all right" we can begin to seek the power and the spiritual strength within that will help us to ease the pain of our anguish and deal with our grief.

DON'T LET YOUR TEARS PUT OUT THE LIGHT

A poet once compared grief to the quenching of stars, one by one extinguished until there was darkness. Is this what you are doing?

A man had a little daughter, an only and beloved child. He lived for her. She was his life. When she became ill and the efforts of the most skillful physicians failed to cure her, he became like a man possessed, moving heaven and earth to bring about her recovery. All efforts proved unavailing, and the little child died.

The father's heart was broken. He was totally unconsolable. He became a bitter recluse, shutting himself away from his many friends and refusing every activity that might restore his poise and bring him back to a normal life.

One night he had a dream. He was in heaven and was witnessing a giant pageant of all the little child angels. They were marching in an apparently endless line, past a great white throne. Every white-robed angelic tot carried a candle. He noticed that one child's candle was not lit. Then he saw that the child with the dark candle was his own little girl.

Rushing to her, he took her in his arms, caressed her tenderly, and asked, "How is it, darling, that your candle is not lit?"

The child said, "Father, they often relight it, but your tears always put it out."

Just then he awoke. From that hour on, he was no longer a recluse but began to mingle freely and lovingly with his former friends. No longer would his little darling's candle be extinguished by his tears.

It is time now to begin to work through your grief, one step at a time, to ease the pain of the toothache in your heart by identifying yourself with laughter and love, with light and life.

If you are afraid to take the step into the light, and if you doubt whether you can do it, then think about a sign that stands at the highest point on the longest and most hazardous road in the Rockies. Just as the nervous driver approaches this extremely narrow, winding mountain pass he sees a reassuring sign that reads: "Oh, yes, you can! Millions have before you."

One Step at a Time!

Do not be afraid to protest and question—even God.

❧ ☙

Realize that even if your questions were answered,
the pain would be no less.

❧ ☙

Expect some of the physical and psychological
consequences of grief.

❧ ☙

Do not extinguish the light with your tears. Identify
your loved one's memory with laughter and love,
with light and life.

❧ ☙

You have to work through your grief. No one else
can do it for you.

❧ ☙

Know that you can do it. Millions have before you.

3

The Melody of Broken Strings

❧ ❧

Grief and love go hand in hand.
—Union Prayerbook, Central Conference
of American Rabbis

I VISITED A FRIEND who had just lost her husband in an automobile accident. She said, "I'm having terrible trouble with memories. Whenever I think I'm coming out of it and seem to be starting to rebuild my life without Frank, something happens that sets me back.

"When I gave Frank's clothes away to the Goodwill people, I felt guilty, even though I saved some things that had sentimental value. You know, just little things that reminded me of him.

"Sometimes I find myself going to the drawer and taking out his pipe and tobacco pouch, and all the grief comes flooding back. How could I discard our wedding pictures, or the snapshots taken when we were on trips? I find myself looking at them over and over again. I guess I'm just a compulsive masochist or something. I know I'm going to suffer, but I can't help it.

"What am I going to do about my memories, not only

the sad ones, but the happy ones, too? Even music. Frank and I used to go to concerts and listen to records at home, holding hands, never saying a word, but feeling complete with the beautiful oneness of our quiet, tranquil love. Now I don't go to concerts or listen to records anymore because music reminds me of Frank and all the music has gone out of my heart."

Would You Like to Forget?

Have you ever felt this way? If you have, then you will probably be able to understand and relate to the Greek legend about a woman who approached the River Styx to be ferried across to the region of departed spirits:

> Charon the ferryman reminded her that it was her privilege to drink of the waters of Lethe and thus forget the life she was leaving. This seemed to be a wonderful idea and she said, "I will forget how I have suffered." Added Charon, "Yes, but you will also forget how you have rejoiced."
>
> She said, "I will forget my failures." The old ferryman added, "And also your victories." She continued, "I will forget how I have been hated." Charon hastened to add, "And also how you have been loved."
>
> When she considered the matter, she decided not to drink the Lethe potion, but to retain her memory, even of the bad, that she might never forget the good. She now knew that to forget the heartache of sorrow is to forget the heartthrobs of joy and love.

It is true that without memory we would not recall the hurt, the pain, the anguish of bereavement. But without memory we would not recall the tenderness, beauty, and goodness, and the wondrous gift of love that was, and still is, ours. Grief and love go hand in hand. Without love, no tears would fall—but without love how poor we would be!

What if we had the power to erase from our minds all remembrance of the hurt, the loss, and the suffering we have experienced because of the passing of dear ones? Then we would also have to erase from our minds and hearts the memory of their goodness and tenderness, their laughter and their love. If there is remembrance of beauty and love, there must be remembrance of pain. Would we want to surrender that pain and, at the same time, surrender the memory of everything they meant to us? I believe that if we had the choice, most of us would rather remember, even the pain.

YOUR NAME IS WRITTEN UPON MY HEART

There was a man named David Levy whose sole ambition from an early age was to be immortalized in human history. How this man wanted his name to be known!

When he was a youngster David Levy carved his name on a tree in the woods and he thought, "Now, everybody who goes by this tree will know David Levy." His family moved away, and years later when he came back and went to the tree, he discovered that it had been chopped down. His name was gone.

He then decided to chisel his name into a rock perched on the top of a cliff. But when he came back again many years later, he discovered that the rain and elements had chipped the letters away and his name could no longer be deciphered.

In time, he became a successful businessman and he declared, "I will erect an imposing building and I will call it 'The David Levy Building.'" And so he did, but some years later, a fire burned the structure to the ground.

Discouraged and despairing of ever perpetuating his name, he began to share his means with worthy causes and needy people. One day he went to the ward of a children's hospital and brought toys for the poor children. One little girl looked up with gratitude in her eyes and said, "Mr. Levy, I will never forget you." He smiled as he answered, "Thank you, dear. That is sweet of you to say but I'm afraid that after a while, you will." "Oh no," the child responded. "I will never forget you because, you see, your name is written upon my heart."

Those who live in the hearts of dear ones left behind can never truly die. This may be what the prophet Isaiah meant when he said, "Thy dead shall live, my dead bodies shall arise—awake and sing, ye that dwell in the dust—for thy dew is as the dew of light, and the earth shall bring to life the shades" (Isaiah 26:19). The dead do live, every time they are remembered.

It has been said that "it is given to love to keep its own eternally." At times the dead are closer to us than the living. The wisdom and love they gave us still protect and help us in difficult situations. Sometimes we do not fully understand their love until it has become a memory.

Can we ever lose the memories of the years we shared with those we loved? Can we ever lose the goodness and the love they engendered in our hearts and minds? Can we ever lose the thoughts and feelings of laughing together, crying together, quarreling and making up, the touch of their hands, the sounds of their voices, the warmth and tenderness of their devotion? We would not be worthy of love and all it gives if, when it is taken from us, we did not miss it. We could not even speak of losing love if we had not possessed it. Memories are precious reminders that the dead are not lost.

"Alas for those who cannot sing, but die with all their music in them." The dead live again when we sing the songs they never sang. They live again when we orchestrate love, the song of songs, into the symphony of life. They live again when memory inspires us to search for truth, appreciate beauty, combat evil, suffering, and injustice in the world, serve worthy causes, and attain the maturity and sensitivity that will enable us to love and be loved.

HAVE WE FORGOTTEN HOW TO REMEMBER?

Perhaps you can recall an old song written by Irving Berlin, called "Remember." The song ends with the words, "But you forgot to remember."

I wonder how often we forget to remember what we owe to our dear ones. How often do we forget to remember what they taught us, the ideals and principles that were so dear and important to them?

It was an icy dawn on February 3, 1943. The American troopship *Dorchester*, carrying hundreds of American soldiers, plowed through the black, churning waters off Greenland. Then came a terrible explosion. A torpedo from a Nazi submarine ripped into the heart of the *Dorchester*. Within minutes it was evident that the ship would sink, and in icy waters where no man could survive more than a half hour at most.

You can imagine the confusion, panic, and fear that swept through the hearts of the men. As the decks slanted and the chilly waters rose, the soldiers knew that many of them would die.

There were four young chaplains on the U.S.S.

Dorchester—Clark V. Poling and George L. Fox, Protestants; Johnny P. Washington, Roman Catholic; and Alexander D. Goode, Jewish. As they stood on the slanting, water-sloshed decks with their life belts on, they saw soldiers without any lifesaving equipment. Without a life belt a man was doomed, and even with one his chances of survival were slim unless he could get into a lifeboat.

Without hesitation the four chaplains took off their life belts and gave them to four men. As the ship slid downward these four courageous men of God were seen standing together, hands firmly clasped, praying, "Our Father . . . Who art in heaven . . . hallowed be Thy name . . . Sh'ma Yisrael Adonai Elohenu Adonai Echod . . . Thy Kingdom come . . ."

That was the last ever seen of these young chaplains. Alexander Goode was my classmate. Could I have done what he did? Would I have had the courage? I do not know, but I do not want to ever forget to remember Alexander Goode.

Today as a memorial to these men there stands on the campus of Temple University in Philadelphia a chapel for the students called the Chapel of the Four Chaplains.

I have often wondered just who the four soldiers were who took the life belts. Did they know they were depriving the chaplains of any chance for safety? Or did they think that the chaplains were passing out life belts as a part of their duty? Did these four men survive? Are they living today? If they did survive and are living now, they owe a debt they can never repay to these chaplains. Are they living the kind of life that is worth saving? Are they trying to repay the gift of life by living dedicated lives? Or have they forgotten to remember?

What about us? Are we living grateful or ungrateful lives? Do we allow our dear ones to live again through our gratitude? Have we forgotten to remember?

THE STOREHOUSE OF MEMORY

A young clergyman serving his first parish in a small Midwestern town often sought the advice of a retired minister living there.

On one occasion, he asked, "What would you preach if you knew that you had only one sermon to deliver?"

After a pause the older man replied, "I'd tell the people to get themselves some worthwhile memories!"

Leo Baeck was a theologian and brilliant scholar who suffered in a concentration camp in Germany, remaining with his people to share suffering and anguish rather than accepting a position of honor and security in America. He once said that we should consider what we put into the storehouse of memory. "Let it not be hatred and bitterness," he said, "but let us fill our minds with love, beauty, reverence, and hope."

This from a man who was tortured by the Nazis in the brutal camp of Theresienstadt. This from a man who had every right to protest, cry out in hatred and bitterness against the cruelty of humanity, the seeming passivity of God, and the meaningless mockery of life. Instead, Leo Baeck refused to become a slave to bitterness. He refused to fill his mind with ugliness and sorrow. He chose to fill his mind and heart with compassion, loving kindness, and hope.

Leo Baeck was a slave in a concentration camp, but the Nazis could not imprison his spirit. Fortunately, we are not imprisoned. We are not indentured to the servitude of eternal and painful bereavement. But many of us feel we are slaves held in bondage by the chains of grief, bound to bitterness and hopelessness, all because of what we have put into the storehouse of memory.

Do we think we pay tribute to our dead by excoriating ourselves with guilt, allowing the tear-filled fountains of our souls to overflow? Is this what memory does to us? Is this the most reverent affirmation of our love?

A person's most valuable possession is his or her memory. In nothing else is he or she rich. In nothing else is he or she poor.

It is our choice. With what will we fill the storehouse of our minds? With memories of our fear, loneliness, and sorrow, or with memories of courage, joy, and dignity that honor our beloved?

BOOKS ON THE SHELVES OF THE MIND

There are memories that bless and there are those that curse. There are memories that hurt and others that heal. What kind of memories predominate for you?

There are many books in my library. Some are catalogued and some are not, but I know approximately where each one is, and what each one contains. There are many books on the shelves of my mind, too. These are memories of dear ones I have loved and still love. I can be selective and take down the memories from the shelf of my mind and reread the book of beautiful lives. I do not have to read all the books that disturb and upset me—I choose the ones I want. I can select a book of memory to look at and again experience with gratitude the beauty, the worth, and the loveliness it recalls of those who have wed their souls to the universe.

The choice is ours. We can determine to go on by choosing memories that will help us to live again.

THE BROKEN STRINGS

A little over a century ago, Niccolo Paganini's violin was enchanting the audiences of Europe, thrilling music lovers with the grandeur of its clarion tones. Paganini was gaunt, emaciated, with waxen face and long black hair, and his clumsy movements frequently provoked unrestrained laughter.

During one of his scheduled concerts, it seemed that all the fates were conspiring against him. Paganini limped onto the platform because a nail had run into his heel. As he tuned his violin, both candles fell out of the music box. The audience tittered. After he had played a few bars, one of the strings of his violin broke. The throng laughed. When a second string broke, the laughter was more audible. But when a third string snapped and Paganini continued to draw divine music out of the single remaining string, the audience fell into a deep silence. They forgot his clumsiness and the ridiculous appearance that he made. The music continued despite those broken strings and the melody of the concert with broken strings remained singing through their lives for many years.

Our dear ones are like songs to us, songs we loved and lived. Now they sing no more. The song is over, but does not the melody of love linger on? Memory is the melody of their song of life and love, and as long as we remember them the melody cannot be forgotten, nor can it ever fade away. As long as we remember them, they continue to live because their memories are written upon our hearts.

Many of us suffer with broken hopes, broken hearts, and broken strings. Paganini did not cancel the concert because of three broken strings. He had one string of his violin left.

There are broken strings in our hearts too, but some unbroken strings remain to contribute to the concert of life. When we live again, we transpose cherished memories into the music of divinity. Many others have done it. We can do it too.

One Step at a Time!

If we had the power to forget the bad memories, we also wouldn't be able to remember the good memories.

❧ ☙

Do not put bitterness and hatred, but love and hope into the storehouse of memory.

❧ ☙

We can choose memories that will help us and our departed to live again.

❧ ☙

When we live again, our departed live again. We must try to get back into life, to make music of memories despite the broken strings of our broken hearts.

4

This Too Shall Pass

❧ ❧

*And love our loved ones with an added
tenderness, because the days of love are
short.*

—Rauschenbusch

ALL THAT EXISTS IS in the process of changing from
being to becoming. Nothing in life remains static.
Everything progresses or regresses. Everything in life
is dynamic and changing.

Over one of the entrances to the Cathedral of Milan,
there is carved a rose, and the inscription: "Beauty
fadeth and wasteth away." Over a second entrance,
there is chiseled a sword, and the inscription: "Pain
ends at last and is no more." Over the central entrance,
there is carved a lamp, and the words: "But the things
of the spirit are for everlasting life."

While we suffer we think that it will never end. When
we are crushed by sorrow and our hearts are torn with
grief, we think that it will be this way forever. No one
can convince us that the wounds will heal. It is difficult
to believe that the agony will abate.

When we think and believe this way, we should

consider the legend of King David and the inscription on his ring—it reaches through the millennia of time and space to speak to our sorrowing hearts:

> David was a man of many moods. Once when he was despondent, he called upon the court jeweler and commanded him, "Inscribe something upon a ring that will lift me up when I am melancholy, convinced that there can never be any hope of a better tomorrow.
>
> "When I am successful, convinced that I will ever be triumphant, exalted and joyous, let the inscription bring me down from my exaltation.
>
> "This is your challenge. There must be but one inscription for both joy and sorrow."
>
> The jeweler pondered the matter for many months. What could he inscribe on a ring that would help the king lift himself from his despondency and, at the same time, bring him down when he climbed to the heights of exaltation and triumph?
>
> He could think of nothing. One day as he walked through the palace gardens, he saw the youthful Solomon. The jeweler asked, "What can I inscribe upon a ring that will help the King lift himself up when he is in despair, and bring him down when he is victorious and triumphant?"
>
> Solomon replied, "Inscribe upon the ring these words: Gam Zu Ya-avor (This too shall pass)."
>
> When the king looked upon the inscription, he knew that both sorrow and joy are not forever. When he was exalted and joyful, he looked upon the ring and moderated his exaltation. When he was despondent, he looked upon the ring and knew "this too shall pass."

We, too, oscillate between joy and sorrow, despair and hope. This is the human condition. Today we suffer in our bereavement and are devastated and depleted by our sorrow. To believe that we will not always suffer so and that there can be a new tomorrow does not detract from our love for those who have died.

Renoir, the great French artist, suffered from rheumatism in his hands during the latter years of his life. He painted by being placed in a chair, which was then moved as he directed. As he applied the paint to the canvas, the intensity of his suffering caused perspiration to cover his brow. Yet he persisted and continued to paint masterpieces. One day his disciple, Matisse, pleaded, "Why torture yourself to do more?" Gazing at his favorite canvas, Renoir replied, "The pain passes, but the beauty remains."

When you are convinced that suffering is eternal, think about the words inscribed upon the ring of King David—"This too shall pass." And remember Matisse and know that the pain will ease and gently fade away, but the beauty will remain forever.

LEARNING FROM GRIEF

King David learned an important lesson about the transience, brevity, and dynamism of human life. Many others have prayed with the Psalmist: "So teach us to number our days that we may get us a heart of wisdom" (Ps. 90:12). Life is brief and fleeting, like the shadow of a bird in flight. How many of us have cried out, "Why didn't I take more time to love my dear ones when they were living? No, I was too busy with so many things that I didn't give priority to love, and now it's too late." We berate and excoriate ourselves for our selfishness and neglect, but this does not help the dead, nor does it help us.

We still have dear ones who are precious to us. We should learn from our grief to rearrange our priorities for those who are still with us, knowing that the days of love are short, and that these months and years that we have together now, "these too shall pass."

What if we knew we all had only five minutes more to live? A wise teacher said that if this were so, every telephone booth in the world would be jammed with people desperately calling others to tell them they loved them. If we believe this is true, then we should not wait until "sometime" or "some day."

We lament the fleeting days and sigh, "Where in the world has the time gone?" What have we done to fill those days with an abundance of our love? It is only these short intervals of genuine communication between ourselves and our dear ones, the moments of true sharing with others, that help us understand the brevity of life and the timelessness of love.

How do we make the years of our lives meaningful? How do we really come alive? I've asked myself that question many times. Now I am asking you. What if you had, not five minutes, but only one more year to live? Some of us would pursue all the pleasures of life, traveling and trying to cram a lifetime of living into that year. Then there would be moments when we would try to assess what is important and what is unimportant, to separate and distinguish that which is temporary and transitory from that which is abiding, real, and meaningful. Some would take time to look at a flower, a tree, or the glory of a sunset. Many would take time for love, time for compassion, time to bring joy and fulfillment to others. That which was so vital and so important before might become unimportant and trivial. That which was secondary and peripheral might become primary and essential.

Being fuses into becoming; life is in constant change. Everything that is grows or decays. Whatever we feel or see is subject to the dynamism of life. Whomever we love, and whoever loves us, will never remain static or permanent. Our priorities can change us, and we can change our priorities now, while there is still time.

Life is particularly precious and sacred to those who have walked through the valley of the shadow of death and have recovered. I have asked many, "What was the most important lesson you learned?" Invariably I receive the same answer: "I learned to establish priorities." Most of them meant that they had learned the importance of that which was once so unimportant— dear ones, friends, beauty, love, faith, prayer, God, compassion for others, and the sanctity of life. One man put it this way: "I've learned the unimportance of that which was once so important to me. When I thought I was going to die, I no longer cared about my business, money, stocks, bonds, or real estate. I saw these things as trivial. Above all, I learned to appreciate life. I once took it for granted. I don't anymore."

Bernard Baruch, the advisor to many United States presidents, was once conferring with Franklin Delano Roosevelt. Mr. Roosevelt told Baruch that his mother was ill, but that he was so pressed by the urgent business of the nation that he was postponing a visit to her for a week to ten days. Mr. Baruch recalled that he replied, "Mr. President, I'm older than you. I can never cease to regret the times I could have been with my mother and wasn't." As a result of this conversation, Mr. Baruch said Roosevelt paid an immediate visit to his mother. If we only knew all the past and future regrets we could prevent by showing our love now!

THE TIME OF OUR LIFE

Time is not a commodity that may be bought or sold. It is a gift for us to use as we wish. We are given the freedom of will to use it wisely or unwisely; the time of our life, too, is a gift given to us on loan. It is not given to us in perpetuity; there is no guarantee as to its longevity. It is a temporary loan that we must return to the rightful owner upon an expiration date that is unknown. There is no court of appeals when the loan expires, because it is entrusted to us by the highest of all courts of appeals.

In ancient sacred literature there is the story of Beruriah, the wife of Rabbi Meir, who found their two sons dead.

> With unspeakable sorrow, she covered them and awaited her husband's return from the synagogue. When Rabbi Meir asked to see his sons, his wife said, "In time, but first I must ask your judgment on an immediate matter. Two precious jewels were given to a man on loan. What should he do when the rightful owner asks for them to be returned?"
>
> Her husband answered, "Of course they must be returned to their rightful owner upon demand."
>
> She then took his hand and led him into the room where their two sons lay dead. When he screamed in his sorrow, Beruriah put her arms around him and said, "My husband, did you not say that the two jewels should be returned to the rightful owner? Our sons were the two jewels given to us by God. Now God, the rightful owner, has demanded their return. Should we not give them back with gratitude for the time we had them?"

TO LIVE AND LET DIE

Profound wisdom was attributed to Solomon, King David's son, who wrote in the book of Ecclesiastes:

> To every thing there is a season and time to every purpose under heaven:
> A time to be born and a time to die . . .
> A time to kill, and a time to heal;

A time to break down, and a time to build up;
A time to weep and a time to laugh,
A time to mourn and a time to dance,
A time to keep, and a time to let go. . . .

Isn't it time for us to heed what he taught? In our grief we have killed our joy and our happiness. This is the time to begin our healing. We have found the time to break down, to weep, to mourn, and to keep. Now is the time to build up, laugh, dance, and let go.

Paul McCartney composed a popular song called "Live and Let Die." The lyrics are somewhat cynical and bitter; they urge us to live it up, have a great time, and if we die through dissipation and drugs, then let die.

In a very different sense we do have to learn to live and let die. I'm referring to those who hold on to their grief—those who do so on purpose, and those who do so unintentionally because they simply cannot help it. They never let their dear ones go. They substitute themselves for the dead and die vicariously while they are still living.

How simple and yet how profound is the truth that we have to *live* for our dear ones and not *die* for them. We must speak silently to them, saying, "Because you were with me music has more melody, and that which was once beautiful is more beautiful. Because of your touch, your life, and your memory, my heart is more sensitive and my soul is more compassionate. Because of you, my life is ever more meaningful and sacred." This is what it means to live and let die. This is what Solomon meant when he wrote, "God hath made everything beautiful in its time."

Life and death, joy and sorrow, youth and old age, spring and winter—everything is beautiful in its time.

Even death is beautiful in its time. To see this, we must dry the tears that obscure our vision and look again at the world with eyes that are made brighter and sharper by the clarity of love.

TO FORGIVE WITHOUT FORGETTING

It is important to forgive ourselves, and also to forgive those who have died. Forgive the dead? This may seem to be an outrageous thought.

A remarkable rabbinic statement made over 2500 years ago asks, "Why do we remember our dead on the Day of Atonement? Because the dead, too, need atonement." Incredible as it may seem to us, even the dead need to be forgiven.

Perhaps it does not apply to you, but there are some who have not forgiven the dead. As irrational as it may seem, deep down there may be anger that they left us when we needed them so. Why did they leave us all alone? Why did they take so much love away from us? Sometimes our resentment leads to guilt and depression.

A woman came to see me because she was depressed over the loss of her mother. She spoke about how much she loved and missed her. She told me of the beautiful qualities of her mother's character, the goodness of her mother's life. How could she go on? She was despondent at the thought of living without her mother. She doubted whether she could ever be the same or ever get over her loss.

The woman went into a deeper depression. Her doctor prescribed drugs to combat the depression, but she continued to be despondent. She went to a psychiatrist for therapy, but nothing seemed to help.

Then something very unexpected happened. While

I was visiting her she asked me to pray with her. As I did, she broke down and sobbed saying, "Help me, please help me, to get these terrible thoughts out of my mind!" I asked her to explain. With difficulty she told me that she resented the fact that her mother had left a larger amount of money to her sister than to herself. "I don't mean to be so selfish or envious, but all through the years," she said, "my sister lived out of town and seldom called or wrote to my dear mother. I was the one who took care of her when she was sick. I was the one who drove her around and shopped for her, and yet she left more money to my sister than she did to me."

When the woman forgave her mother and forgave herself for her resentments, she was able to come up from her depression. She was helped by the realization that both life and the days of love are fleeting. She was helped by the recognition that we are all fallible human beings who make mistakes.

A TIME TO FORGIVE—OURSELVES

Stop for a moment and think—is it possible that you need to forgive yourself? When we are in grief we feel guilty, and often we reproach ourselves for things we did or should have done.

A three-year-old child drowned in the family's swimming pool. He had chased a ball and fallen into the pool. The father said he would never forgive himself. "I spanked Danny this morning. The last thing I ever did with Danny was not to put my arms around him and love him, but use my arms and my hands to hurt him."

The mother cried out, "It's all my fault. I am to blame. I should have been right there with him instead of in the house taking a bath. I warned him about going near the pool, but he didn't listen. He was only a child, a little boy running after a ball, but I'm an adult, and I should have watched him more carefully. I should have been responsible. I am to blame. I'll never forgive myself as long as I live."

"I did this to him," another mother confessed over the death of her son. "He had the sniffles. He was pale. I could see he was sick. It was over a week before I called the doctor. It was all my fault. I let him get worse, and he died. I'm responsible for the death of my own boy!"

A father telephoned his fifteen-year-old daughter who was at a boarding school in another city to tell her that her mother had just died after a prolonged illness. The girl screamed, "I did it. I killed my own mother. I didn't even want to visit her in the hospital because of the smell of ether, vomit, and bedpans. It made me sick. I even asked to be sent out of town to school so I wouldn't have to be close to her. And I did more— something terrible. I hated her. I hated her because she wasn't like other mothers who did things and went places with their daughters, mothers who helped their daughters get dressed for parties and dates. I hated her because she was dying and I believed that I would in- herit the same disease and die, too. I even prayed to God that she should die and that you would remarry and give me a healthy mother. God heard my prayers and made her die. I killed her! I killed her!"

How many are suffering from this misplaced guilt, these self-inflicted tortures? Women who have had abortions. Men who have been away when a loved one died. Wives and husbands who have prayed that a mate be allowed to die and not suffer anymore. We all have to learn to forgive ourselves.

A man was disconsolate because he had signed permission for the doctors to perform surgery on his elderly father. When the father died on the operating table, the son cried, "I shouldn't have signed it. He was too old and too weak. I'm responsible for the death of my own father and I'll never forgive myself."

Self-blame and self-recrimination are part of grieving. Sometimes our thoughts are unreasonable as we see ourselves as executioners, or accessories to unpremeditated murder. A distraught mother whose child had died after a lingering battle with leukemia literally tore at her own flesh as she repeated over and over again, "I did it! I did it! Sarah died because of my sins. God made her die to punish me. I'm the one who should have died. I'm the one they should put in the grave. I'm responsible for the death of my own darling daughter!"

Have you ever said this or thought this in the privacy of your mind? If so, how can you believe in a God of love, a Heavenly Father whose compassion is without limit? If I believed that God took the life of an innocent child as a means of punishing the mother for her wrongdoings, I would become a militant atheist, crusading against a God of hate. But I do not believe that God demands that we make vicarious atonement for the sins of others. I do not believe that God is so cruel that He would inflict sickness and death upon a child or anyone else as punishment for the sins or wrongdoings of another.

It is fortunate that most of us do not and cannot remain very long on the peaks or in the valleys of life. We usually move to the plateaus. Despite ourselves, our joys are ephemeral and transitory, and even the sorrow of bereavement and the agony of grief yield to the inevitability of change.

During the years of my ministry and counseling, I have learned that Dr. Eric Lindemann was correct when he said that guilt usually accompanies grief. It may be undeserved, repressed, or delayed guilt, but most of us experience it to some degree. We should examine ourselves in the light of reason and recognize that we are not that guilty. We should forgive ourselves when there is something to forgive—and even when there is nothing to forgive. It is time to pardon and release ourselves. It is time to return to the realities of life.

As God forgives, so we must forgive, both the dead and ourselves. As God has forgiven us for our mortal limitations and fallibilities, so we must forgive. We must rid ourselves of our locked-in guilt, anger, hurt, and resentments. We must bury the hurt, and take a last look at the real or imagined guilt we feel before we enter it in the tomb of yesterday.

We must yield in quiet resignation to the reality of life and death, recognizing that our loved ones were not perfect, just as we are not perfect. We need the humility to realize that perfection is reserved for God, the humility that allows us to accept our fallibility as human beings. This will help us to say of our feelings of guilt and self-reproach, "This too shall pass."

We can then love our loved ones who are still alive with an added tenderness, because the days of love are short. When mourning comes, we should be reminded that there is a time to hold and a time to let go. Believing that God has made everything beautiful in its time, now is the time when we should *love* and let die. Now is the time when we should *live* and let die.

One Step at a Time!

When you are convinced that your grief will never end, think about the inscription on the ring of King David: "This too shall pass."

Reassess your priorities.

"There is a time to keep and a time to let go." Say goodbye to your dead so that the healing process may begin.

Forgive the departed and forgive yourself.

Stop torturing yourself with deserved or undeserved guilt.

Take some positive action on behalf of the living.

Love your loved ones now with an added tenderness, because the days of love are short.

5

Putting Yourself Inside Out

❧ ❧

If I am for myself alone, what am I?
—Hillel

S O MANY WHO ARE GRIEVING are weary of empty
words, pious platitudes, and well-meant but irritat-
ing assurances that "you will get over it."

Actually we do not just "get over it." We never really
get over the loss of dear ones, nor should we. Precious
memories will always remain as sacred reminders of
the gifts of love. What we want is to work through the
pain and suffering caused by our grief. "Getting over it"
has the implication of being finished with it. We want
to get over our mental and emotional anguish, but we
never want to get over our memories.

Time does not heal by itself. We must do more than
wait for its calming and healing effects. In order to
restructure our lives, it is necessary for us to do something, to take action, to make the effort to go beyond
ourselves and put ourselves inside out to achieve what
Dr. Karl Menninger, the eminent psychiatrist, calls
"the vital balance."

Time does give us the opportunity to deal with our grief, to get out of ourselves and go beyond ourselves to others. Through our inner potential we find strength, not only to help ourselves, but to help others. The magnificent paradox works the other way, too—when we strengthen others, we strengthen ourselves; when we help others, we help ourselves; when we lose ourselves in the concern for others, we find and fulfill ourselves.

This is an ancient truth taught by religious teachers and sages and now reaffirmed by modern psychologists, physicians, psychiatrists, and those who are doing research in glandular and hormonal function and dysfunction.

Dr. Hans Selye also attests to the importance of the vital balance for physical, emotional, and mental health. To some, Dr. Selye may sound more like a clergyman than a scientist when he calls for "altruistic egotism," achieved by the maintaining of a healthy ego and concern for self, and then going beyond self to others for gratitude, love, and greater self-fulfillment.

This internationally celebrated physician, the recipient of a Nobel Prize for his scientific research, is calling for a spiritual homeostasis (balance) to deal with the emotional suffering of grief. He is urging us to utilize our inner resources to work through our bereavement by going beyond ourselves to others. In other words, he is advising the bereaved to put themselves inside out.

How startling and significant it is that over two thousand years before Hans Selye was born, the Hebrew sage Hillel asked, "If I am not for myself, who will be for me? But if I am for myself alone, what am I? And if not now, when?" Dr. Hans Selye and Dr. Karl Menninger are now advocating what Joshua of Nazareth and Hillel of Judaea taught in ancient days.

To do our grief work, it is essential that we first try to discover and utilize the power within ourselves, and then get outside of ourselves to others—not in the future, not when the pain of sorrow may be dulled by time, but now. ("If not now, when?")

GRIEF WORK

"Life goes on . . . I forget just why," Edna St. Vincent Millay wrote. It is from this point that grief work begins. Grief work involves the recall and sifting of past memories. The desire to be with the deceased is replaced by a desire to fulfill their ambitions and ideals. Remember that you have to work out your grief. The important words are "work out."

Most religions provide us with a ritualized structure and meaningful ceremonies that are helpful to observe in working out grief. Each religious discipline offers prescribed mourning customs and traditions we would be wise to follow. The rites of bereavement, the mourning before the funeral, the funeral itself, as well as the traditions to be observed following the funeral all help us to begin to work out our grief.

An inconsolable man once asked me if there is any way of speeding up the grief work. Professionals have attempted to help by encouraging anger, explaining the grief process; they have tried persuasion, prayer, even hypnosis. But these therapies have seldom met with success. The best and most effective kind of help is self-healing. The grieving person must face up to his negative reaction to change. He must confront his own fallibility and recognize that no one really knows why life is as it is. He must be helped to understand that prolonged grief is often the result of excessive isolation, immaturity, self-centeredness, self-pity, and the inability to let go of the past and redirect himself to the present and the future.

The first indications of grief work appear when the grief-stricken begin to ask themselves, "How can I react differently? What shall I do and what can I do to change my morbid behavior?" Grief work starts when the bereaved begin to change their focus from self to others. Friends may be supportive. Professional therapists and clergy may help. But in essence, each person has to work out his or her grief.

Dr. Eric Lindemann* has shown in his work on grief and grieving that the evaluation of the experience of grief is the only way a person can help himself. This process, Lindemann believes, brings about greater self-awareness and self-understanding.

THE FIRST STEPS

Physical activity is extremely important in times of stress caused by grief. Inactivity promotes brooding. People in very stressful situations create excessive amounts of hormones and other chemicals that cause the organs, and especially the circulatory system, to speed up and even race. Activity is necessary to keep this acceleration from becoming harmful.

A minister tells of how he helped a congregant begin to do his grief work by urging him to complete painting the basement he had left unfinished since his wife's death five months prior. The two men put on old clothes and worked together for two hours. It was a beginning.

The activity does not have to be anything unusual or

---

* Eric Lindemann, The Symptomatology and Management of Acute Grief, *American Journal of Psychiatry* 101 (1944), 141–48.

extraordinary. It may be washing clothes, ironing, mowing the lawn, raking leaves, fixing a lamp or a leaky faucet, browsing at an antique shop, taking clothes to the dry cleaners, buying a new dress or suit, going to the beauty parlor or barber shop, or shopping at the supermarket. Some of these trivial chores or activities may elicit memories of the dead, but the risk must be taken and faced. Every commonplace or routine activity is a step forward. It is important that you set a number of short-term goals for yourself. Make a list of some of the things you should be doing, and try to do at least one every day.

Although it may be difficult, the next activity should be an overt reaching out to relatives and friends. Seeing them may be a sign of working out your grief and taking another step into the world. Do not try to go on bravely and heroically alone. Others may have telephoned you. Now it is your turn. A simple telephone call to them will help you to start putting yourself inside out.

The biggest step of all is when you try to help others around you who need your help. If they are grieving, they need your presence; they need you to be there. They will know that you understand and sympathize. By giving comfort and strength to others, you will not only put yourself inside out, but you will also experience a greater calmness and peace within yourself.

A Funeral at Four O'Clock

Somehow sorrow makes us all the more aware of how much we need each other. There are times when we think, "I stand alone. I don't need anybody. I can take care of myself. I am independent. I am self-sufficient. I can handle it all." Then there are times when we know we cannot stand or walk alone. Sorrow makes us aware of how much we need our friends and our loved ones to stand with us, to weep with us, and to strengthen us in our sorrow.

A wealthy man once said he would divide his fortune among his true friends if he only knew who they were. He was suspicious of everyone who offered friendship, thinking that their only interest was in his money. He drove everyone away who offered him love and support.

At last, alone and friendless, the old man died during a winter blizzard. His last request was that his funeral be held at four o'clock in the morning.

Three men and one woman appeared at four o'clock on the bitter cold morning to stand red-eyed and grief-stricken beside his grave. When his will was read it directed that his estate be divided equally among those who attended his funeral.

This man had friends, but he did not know it. He had friends but he did not enjoy them. He made his friends rich through his death, but he never really shared with them during his life. He was never able to put himself inside out. Can you?

THE SACKCLOTH WITHIN

Teilhard de Chardin, the French philosopher and theologian, once said that the most important event in the evolution of man took place when "the creature turned the mirror of reflection upon himself." If this is true, then the second greatest event was when man turned the mirror upon his fellowmen and discovered himself in them.

To discover ourselves in others is a necessary part of our grief work. It convinces us that others also grieve, hurt, and suffer loneliness and the pain of bereavement. We then realize that we are not alone in our sorrow.

Almost all of us are familiar with the biblical verse, "Thou shalt love thy neighbor as thyself," but few, if any of us, are able to live up to this admonition. Our English translation is neither a correct nor literal translation of the Hebrew text, which reads: "Love thy neighbor, for he is as yourself." This translation is more feasible and reasonable. We should love our neighbor because he has the same limitations, the same frustrations, weaknesses, and sorrows, the same hopes and dreams and strengths that we have.

In ancient times those who were bereaved would wear sackcloth as a token of their affliction or as a sign of their mourning. Whenever such a person came into view, lowly and dejected, adorned in sackcloth, others would immediately recognize the sign of suffering and would treat the individual with consideration and compassion.

Today, those who suffer or grieve do not wear sackcloth upon their bodies; they are wearing sackcloth within. They have some private sorrow, some personal burden that they carry through a lifetime. Few are aware of it. People do not look upon them with understanding or with compassion, for they are not wearing visible signs of sorrow. Their sackcloth is worn within.

We often look upon others with a great deal of envy. We see the smiling faces of the successful and the powerful and as we compare our own lot to theirs, we feel that life has cheated us. They have so much, and we have so little. We have our sorrows and our burdens, but they have only contentment, joy, and inexpressible happiness. How often we do not know! How often we are wrong!

In the Book of Kings we read of the great famine that spread in Israel when it was besieged by Ben Hadad, the king of Aram. As the king of Israel was passing by, "there cried a woman unto him, saying: 'Help me, O King.' And he said: 'If the Lord do not help thee, whence shall I help thee?' Then the woman told the king of her great sorrow—the loss of her son. And it came to pass that when the king heard the words of the woman, he tore his garments in grief. The people looked, and behold, they saw that beneath his outer garments, he had sackcloth within." Even the king of Israel had his secret sorrow.

THE EMPTY HALL OF SORROW

There is a legend of how Alexander of Macedon consoled his own mother when he knew that his death was near. He wrote her a letter:

"My mother, remember that all earthly things are transitory and that your son was not a small king but a great king. Wherefore you are not to bear yourself like the mother of a little king, but like the mother of a great king.

"After my death command a great hall to be built and command furthermore that on a given day all the princes of the empire shall come thither and be merry and be of good cheer. Cause it to be proclaimed that none is to come who has suffered any ill, for the joy at that feast shall be a pure and perfect joy and shall not be darkened by the thoughts of any concerning any sorrow that has come upon him."

When her son died, she acted exactly according to his will. She had a magnificent hall built and she named the day on which the princes were to come to the feast.

When the appointed day came she was prepared for many, many people. Not a single soul came. She asked the wise men of the court, "What is the meaning of this? Why do not the guests come to this great hall which I have caused to be built?"

The answer she received was this: "Dear Queen, you issued the command that none should come who has suffered any grief or any ill. But there is no such human being in the whole world, and therefore there is no guest who could come."

This consoled the mother of the great king. She was not alone in her grief.

EMPATHIC CONCERN

We must turn to others if we are to return to the world. Sigmund Freud understood this when he wrote that mourning is not just the reaction to the loss of a loved person, but the process of withdrawing interest from that person and transferring it to another. He did not mean that we erase the memories of those we love, but rather that we find others with whom we can share sorrow, joy, and mutual concerns.

When we share we begin to diminish our pain and contribute to our healing. When we go beyond ourselves to others, we enrich the spiritual treasury of our beings. When we give to others, we give even more to ourselves. This is not some kind of "Pollyanna" philosophy; this is not an over-sweet theology that cloys. It is real, practical, and true. It is a requisite for putting your grief to work.

One story from Hasidic lore talks of Moshe Lieb of Sasov who taught us how to love our fellow man.

A peasant taught me what is true love of fellow man. The peasant was sitting in an inn drinking with a companion. Suddenly he turned to his friend and asked: "Ivan, do you love me?"

"I love you very much."

"If you love me, tell me what gives me pain?"

"How would I know that?"

"If you don't know what gives me pain, how can you say you love me?"

To love one's fellow man, Moshe Lieb taught, is to know what gives him pain and to bear the burden of his sorrow. It is told of Moshe Lieb that whenever he saw anyone else's suffering, either of spirit or body, he shared it so earnestly that the other's suffering became his own.

Someone once expressed his astonishment at the sage's capacity to share in another's troubles. "What do you mean share?" said the rabbi. "It is my own sorrow; how can I help suffer it?"

To Moshe Lieb someone else's pain was his own. "When do I truly love my neighbor?" he asked. "When his pain is my sorrow. If someone comes to you and asks your help, you should not turn him away with pious words, saying, 'Have faith! Take your troubles to God. He will help you.' No! You should act as if there were no God, as if there were only one person in the world who could help this man—you."

We take a step out of grief and into the world when we sympathize with others. Yet sympathy is not enough. Sympathy is being sorry for another; it means pity and compassion. If we are to take an even longer step and put ourselves inside out, we need more than sympathy—we need empathic concern.

Empathy is feeling compassion for another, identifying, seeing ourselves in the place and condition of another. Empathic concern requires action. It motivates us to do something for another. It means sharing and helping.

From the legends of the past, we read about a woman

who learned about the suffering and grief of others, and through empathic concern, did something about it.

A sorrowing woman went to a wise man with the heartrending plea that he return to her an only son whom she had just lost. He told her that he would try to comply with her request on one condition: She would have to bring to him a mustard seed taken from a home entirely free from sorrow.

The woman set out on her quest. Years elapsed, and she did not return. One day the wise man chanced upon her, but he hardly recognized her, for now she looked so radiant. He greeted her and then asked her why she had never kept their appointment.

"Oh," she said in a tone of voice indicating that she had completely forgotten about it, "well, this is what happened. In search of the mustard seed, I came into homes so burdened with sorrow and trouble that I just could not walk out. Who better than I could understand how heavy was the burden they bore? Who better than I could offer them the sympathy they needed? So I stayed on in each home as long as I could be of service.

"And," she added apologetically, "please do not be angry, but I never again thought about our appointment."

Six-year-old Mary was late coming home. When her mother asked her why, she said, "Susie broke her doll, and I stopped to help her cry." If we would only take the time to stop long enough to help someone else cry, it would ease the pain of our own grief and help us work through our own troubles.

Sympathy has been defined as "your pain in my heart." Empathic concern is doing something about that pain. Will you stop long enough in your grief to help someone cry, laugh, and live again?

A lone traveler was crossing mountain heights of un-
trodden snow. He struggled bravely against the urge for
sleep which weighed down his eyelids, for he knew that
if he fell asleep, death would be inevitable.

Just then his foot struck against a heap lying across
the path. Stooping down, he found it to be a human
body half buried in the snow. The next moment he held
the body in his arms and was rubbing the frozen man's
limbs.

The effort to restore another to life brought back to
himself warmth and energy, and was the means of saving both men.

In Whittier's words, "Heaven's gate is shut to him
who comes alone/Save thou a soul, and it shall save
thine own."

MUSIC AT MIDNIGHT

Earlier we discussed memory as a melody of broken
strings. The poet George Herbert used the phrase
"music at midnight" to express the importance of putting ourselves inside out. Music at midnight—a strange
expression—and yet we believe that in this phrase we
can find a source of inspiration that may hearten and
sustain us when mourning comes.

Consider the biblical passage: "And it came to pass
at midnight, when the Lord smote the firstborn of
Egypt, and there was a great cry of sorrow that
echoed throughout the land" (Ex. 12:29). The sages
taught that midnight, which is neither today nor tomorrow, an almost neutral interval in time, can be the
occasion not only for sorrow, but for the soul-searching and communion with God. As the Psalmist has
said: "I will rise and praise the Lord at midnight"
(Psalm 119:62).

To George Herbert, midnight meant something else. He said that we all must have memories to draw upon, spiritual investments to use when we are in need.

We all think in terms of savings, of investments for the future. We try to put away earnings and resources that we may draw upon in physical or material need when we are ill, old, or unable to continue our work. Do we ever think of making spiritual investments or of earning beautiful memories that we may draw upon when our emotional and spiritual supplies seem to be depleted and bankrupt?

One time George Herbert came to a gathering with dirty clothes and in an unkempt condition. When the people began to wonder why Mr. Herbert, who was usually so clean and neat, looked so disheveled, he explained that he had given his clean clothes to a beggar in need. He wanted to help the beggar lift himself from the mud and grime into which he had fallen in hunger and exhaustion.

Herbert said that the thought of what he had done would later "prove music to him at midnight."

Others have interpreted this phrase, "music at midnight," in a different sense, not in terms of sorrow or suffering, or even remembering, but to mean that at the time of greatest darkness courage is often born. Throughout the centuries, brave men and women have been sustained and strengthened by sensitizing their souls to hear the music at midnight.

Such a one was Jeremiah, who cried out: "I have become a laughing stock; all the day everyone mocketh me" (Jer. 20:7ff). And at his hour of abject despair, he heard a voice calling to him, summoning him to prophecy. Activated by a divine compulsion he declared,

"And if I say: I will not make mention of Him nor speak any more in His name, then there is in my heart as it were a burning fire shut up in my bones and I weary myself to hold it in and cannot." He rose out of the dust of despair and went on because his soul heard the music at midnight.

Was there ever a man more miserable than Job, a man who lost his children, his possessions, his good name? As he sat on a dung heap scratching and scraping his loathsome sores, he lamented, "Why died I not from the womb? Why did I not perish at birth?" (Job 3:11). His wife taunted him, saying, "Blaspheme, curse God and die" (Job 2:9). But with an affirmation of faith, Job elevated himself above his misery. Job declared his love of God, saying, "Even though He slay me, yet will I trust in Him" (Job 13:15). Job heard the music at midnight, and he was able to go on.

Father Damien volunteered for service among the lepers on the Hawaiian island of Molokai in 1873. He dressed their sores, washed their bodies, built their homes, made their coffins, and buried their dead. There came the day when his feet were insensitive to pain—the first sign of leprosy. He thought of the comfort he had brought, the faith he had given, the solace and strength that had sustained so many. Henceforth he no longer said, "My brethren," but "We lepers."

He lived on for sixteen more years, and died at the age of forty-nine with spirit unbroken, with faith unshaken, with a gentleness and a goodness apparent even on his withered face. He had listened to the music at midnight.

What are the spiritual investments that we make for our time of need? What offerings do we bring to the altar of our minds and souls? What are our memories of services given to others in need? Do we do anything or serve anyone so that we may listen to music at midnight?

Midnight may remind us of the sorrow and the cry of mourning that echoed throughout the land of Egypt; midnight might mean the signal for liberation and freedom; midnight might mean a new beginning, not only of a day, but of a life. Midnight might mean faith, courage, a storehouse of love, the recollection of service, and gratitude for those who were so dear to us. It may also be a portent of our faith and hope as we confront the challenge of today and respond to the summons of tomorrow to go beyond ourselves and put ourselves inside out.

FIRE IN THE SNOW

Several years ago I read a poem by Winifred Rawlins. It had a strange title: "Fire in the Snow."* The poem touched my being with comfort and sublime assurance:

I came by night where snow lay deep,
All was transfixed in frozen sleep;
I felt a sudden small wind blow,
And saw a fire burn in the snow,
With tongues of crimson throb and leap.

Who gave it life I could not know,
Some hand had kindled its brave show;
I felt its primal laughter steep
My mind in happiness and keep
Me gazing, with no will to go.
Now as I sit and watch you weep,
When knowledge fails and words are cheap,

* "Fire in the Snow," by Winifred Rawlins. Reprinted by permission of the Golden Quill Press, Francestown, New Hampshire.

I'll make a little smoldering glow
Of tenderness, and bid it grow;
When it begins to laugh and leap
I'll light a fire in your snow.

To light a fire in the snow, to make a little smoldering glow of tenderness in the hearts of others can help us to put ourselves inside out.

The poet speaks of sorrow as snow. How many fires do we light in the cold rooms of the human soul? How often do we make a little smoldering glow of tenderness and bid it grow in a heart that grieves? How often do we kindle such a glow in the snowy realms of our own hearts through remembrance, through helping others?

I have said it and perhaps you have said it too: "I would like to make a little smoldering glow of tenderness and bid it grow in my heart, and in the hearts of others, but somehow I just haven't been able to do it."

Yes, I can, and you can, too. That is what putting yourself inside out is all about. It is not how long one grieves, but how well one grieves. "Good grief" is the ability to take steps forward and come out of our bereavement with a deeper understanding of human sympathy and empathic concern. "Good grief" not only motivates us to compassion but allows us to convert our compassion into deeds of loving kindness toward others.

Hans Selye and others who have studied the stress caused by grief are convinced that we are under more stress and our sorrow remains more acute when we are unable or unwilling to make decisions. We are able! You and I have the freedom of will to take charge of our lives. God has endowed us with the power to choose, and the ability to control our thoughts, feelings, and actions. But we cannot do this alone. We need God to strengthen us enough to make the decision to put ourselves inside out.

We ask God to help us this day. To what extent are we helping others? We ask God to forgive us this day. To what extent do we forgive others?

Have our hearts become barren and cold, filled with the snow of despair? Do we look upon life as filled with nothing but violence, evil, and selfishness? Are we convinced that human nature is rotten and man is evil? Then we need that little smoldering glow of tenderness to receive and to give.

I hope you will say to yourself and to so many others

> Now as I sit and watch you weep,
> When knowledge fails and words are cheap,
> I'll make a little smoldering glow
> Of tenderness, and bid it grow;
> When it begins to laugh and leap,
> I'll light a fire in your snow.

If we can do that, then we affirm our reverence for life; then we sanctify the memory of our dear ones who are with us no more; then we make of their names fires in the snow, warm and loving benedictions on our lips.

One Step at a Time!

Put your grief to work, starting with little things, an unfinished task or a simple chore undone.

◄§ §►

Look around and put yourself inside out by doing something to help others.

◄§ §►

Each person has to work out his or her grief. Each person must do something, himself or herself.

◄§ §►

Comfort another grieving person by just being there. Stop to help someone cry.

◄§ §►

Express empathic concern by action in behalf of another person.

◄§ §►

Start storing up acts of service that will become "music at midnight."

◄§ §►

Make a little smoldering glow of tenderness in someone's heart and watch it grow.

6

Where There's Hope, There's Life

❦

*Hope seems a star and listening love can
hear the rustle of a wing.*
—Robert Ingersoll

C AN YOU IMAGINE WORKING and living every day
with children who have to face their fear of death?
Doreen Hall Wales did that when she worked in the
City of Hope National Medical Center in Duarte, California, where children's first years are also their last.

When friends ask, "Doreen, how can you take it?"
her answer is that this is the happiest school in which
she ever taught. Happy—when she has to watch her
students die? Happy—when she faces the seemingly
hopeless task of teaching children with terminal ill-
nesses?

Death is always present, and the children know it.
Death is one of their classmates. Death is in their
playacting, their drawings, dreams, and conversations.

Alice, one of the little girls at the school, used humor
as her defense during the last part of her hospital stay.
One day she called from her oxygen tent, "Lend me

your lipstick. At least I want to look pretty." She knew
she was dying and wanted to look pretty when she met
death. Alice realized that death does not have to be
ugly or lonely. It can be quiet, gentle, and even kind.

When she gives parties, Doreen hears children say,
"This is the best party we've ever had." She knows that
for some it may be the last party they will ever have.

How does Doreen take this? Her husband Edward
says that she comes home after a long day more re-
freshed than she ever did from any other school in
sixteen years of teaching. How can this be?

Doreen Hall Wales gives her own answer: "These
children who are beautiful, bright, brilliant, joy-giving,
fun-loving, who don't live long, are like porpoises that
leap and smile at you then disappear forever. My job is
to make their lives as beautiful a leap as I can. I must
keep every child happy each remaining day of his life.
The leap, however brief, must be rich in fulfillment."

She is so busy helping the children live that she has
little time to think about death. She has learned that life
is not measured by the chronological years of a calendar, but by the joy and fulfillment of living. By identifying with a world of dreams, she now understands that
life and death are indivisible. She now knows that death
may be a friend.

You would not have to convince this wonderful
teacher, this sensitive and loving human being, that
"where there's hope, there's life." She knew this when
she watched eight-year-old Elmer peering into a toy
microscope, while elsewhere in the hospital research
doctors were peering into microscopes, too. She could
sense that the two contrasting microscopes—Elmer's
representing learning for learning's sake, and the doctors' representing the application of learning for hu-

manity's sake—symbolized the meaning of hope in a city with that name.

WHERE THERE'S HOPE, THERE'S LIFE

We often say, "Where there's life, there's hope." That is not always true. Dr. Karl Menninger, the famous psychiatrist, insisted that there is even greater truth to the belief that "where there's hope, there's life." Without hope there is little to sustain the will to live. Without hope we are the living-dead marching through the years in a journey to nothingness. We cannot, with impunity to mind, body, or spirit, yield our hope for the future—either for ourselves or for those we love.

We cry aloud. From the voiceless lips of the unreplying dead there comes no word. Do we have the hope that they still live, or that they shall live again? Do we have the hope that we can go on and return to life and living?

POOR BEAR IN A CAGE

The hopelessness of the individual is bound to the hopelessness eloquently or silently spoken by his or her contemporaries. It is also related to the absence of goals. This inevitably results in pessimism about the future and the prospect of a tomorrow that is without attainable purpose or meaning.

Those who experience bereavement are like Robert Frost's "Poor Bear in a Cage," fighting their inward, nervous rage. They pace back and forth, caged in by frustration and hopelessness, yearning to be free. They turn to the burgeoning wonders of science, and the mind encompasses galaxies in space beyond imagination, but they cannot encapsulate or control the tempestuous feelings that surge within them, driving them, goading them, allowing no peace and no hope.

We are able to look at an unseen world through a microscope as the infinitesimal looms in gigantic proportion, but when we are in mourning, we cannot see even the faintest glimmer of hope for the future. We yearn to wrest the secrets of the universe from their esoteric hiding places, but we are unable to grasp even an intimation of the secrets of comfort for our anguished souls. As a consequence, we boldly hurtle down the bastions of long-cherished beliefs and ideals, shaking the standards of our society, tearing at values clothed in sanctity, clawing at the very entrails of respectability. We shock, dethrone, challenge, defy, resist, rebel—anything to express our hurt and our hopelessness. "Who cares? What does anything mean?"

Is this you talking? Is this you thinking, "Even if I face my fear of death and learn to deal with it, what do I have left? I've tried, but it is impossible for me to think about tomorrow or the future without my loved one. I might as well be dead. I'm dead inside—why not all of me? Never again to hear the sound of her voice. Never again to touch and hold her or to make plans for our future together. Now the future is an illusion, a thought, a concept, an anticipated chunk of time—but it can never have meaning or purpose, joy or fulfillment."

IS THERE ANY MEANING?

Death relates to identity and meaning. Whether we want to or not, death compels us to offer some kind of response to the question "Who am I?" The unreal, trance-like quality of our feelings makes us acutely aware of the fuzziness that seems to obscure a sharply defined concept of self.

"Who am I? Is it the real me that experiences the hurt, the shock, the surrealism of death? Could it be that there is 'another self' that feels this way, while the 'real me' is buried somewhere deep in the core of my being?"

That is why it is not abnormal to ask, "Who am I? What am I? What is the meaning of my life?" and especially, "What is the meaning of their death—and some day, my death?"

Swiss psychiatrist Victor Frankl writes in *The Doctor and the Soul,* "Grief has a meaning for the inner biography of man. Grieving for a person in a sense continues his life. The loved one has been lost objectively in empirical time, but he is preserved subjectively. Grief brings him into the mind's present." Therefore, according to Frankl, joy has its friends, but grief its loneliness. That is why there needs to be a journey into the self to search for meaning.

Frankl was comforting a man whose wife had died. "What if you had died first?" asked Frankl. Suddenly the man saw meaning in his loss. He realized that he was better able to withstand the grief than his wife would have been. We need help to find meaning in our loss; we cannot find it alone.

You have cried out of the depths for help—but to whom do you cry? To what shall you lift your eyes and elevate your thoughts? To your fellow man? No, how can he help? Man has become computerized, electronized, and automatized. He says, "I will lift up mine eyes to the test tube. I will lift up mine eyes to the computer. I will lift up mine eyes to the galvanic skin response meter." Do you cry to God, then? Religion has been analyzed, rationalized, demythologized, and paralyzed —how can it help? We are told that a personal God who cares about you and me is either dead or missing in action.

I WILL LIFT MINE EYES UNTO THE MEDICINE CHEST

All right, the requiems have been intoned and the kaddish recited for a dead God. At last we are free from the mandates of divinity only to discover that we have become slaves of hopelessness and despair. Where shall we go? What shall we do?

Once we said, "I will lift up mine eyes unto the mountains, from whence shall come my help. My help cometh from the Lord who made heaven and earth." Now we say, "I will lift up my eyes to the tranquilizers. They will help to soothe me. They will take away the pain of grief. They will give me relief from the pounding of pain deep inside me."

We have tried sermonic sedation and ministerial Miltown to anesthetize our senses. We have turned to Valium, Librium, Elavil, and Tophranil. These have not always helped. We need something more. We need a faith that is predicated on reason, a theology that is grounded in reality and yet enables us to reach for the stars.

Where shall we find this? We have been in the darkness for such a long time. What will help us to turn to the light? Just as Abraham Lincoln once declared, "I have been driven to my knees many times by the realization that I had nowhere else to go," so standing, sitting, lying in bed, or on our knees, we have no alternative but to allow a meaningful faith to help us escape from the cage of hopelessness, to find a new meaning and purpose for our lives by putting ourselves in the spiritual hands of God—the God who can be our light and our salvation.

Hope inclines us to turn to God. Despair inclines us to disbelieve and hide ourselves in corners of pessimism, or escape into bed and pull the covers of fear over our heads. When mourning comes, we need a realistic religious philosophy that can relate death, bereavement, and grief to the totality of life—a religious philosophy that can help us respond to some of the questions raised by our rebelliousness in the face of death.

Martin Buber said, "Real faith does not mean professing what we hold true in a ready-made formula. On the contrary, it means holding ourselves open to the unconditioned mystery which we encounter in every sphere of our life and which cannot be comprised in any formula. It means that, from the very roots of our being, we should always be prepared to live with this mystery as one lives with another."

At a time of hopelessness, the prophet Zachariah proclaimed to his people, "Return to the stronghold, ye prisoners of hope" (Zach. 9:12), and the song that sustained the modern Israelis who suffered the torment of the Holocaust and strengthened their will to live was called "Hatikvah," the Hope.

Hope sustained others in the past and it can sustain us, if we do not defer it, but permit it to enter our thoughts and our feelings.

HELL IS HOPELESSNESS

Dante must have been thinking of us when he wrote in his *Divine Comedy* that at the entrance of hell there is a sign: "Abandon all hope, ye who enter here." He meant that hopelessness is the gateway to hell.

We have entered into our own private hell of hopelessness. Hope for what? Shall I pray and hope for the return of my dear ones who are no longer alive? Shall I hope that I may be liberated from my despair and depression? Should I hope that I will ever get back to work again, feeling as I do?

No, hope will not bring back your dear ones. But hope can help you to come up from your depression, get out of your despair, and return to living. You will not always feel the way you do now. Try to remember a time when you were physically ill with a high temperature, unable to eat, too weak to even get out of bed. You thought you would never get well again—but you did get well. With proper care, rest, healthy thinking, and the resolve and determination to get better, you did get better, almost despite your feelings and your pessimism.

The poet Tennyson, stricken by his personal grief, survived because he was sustained by hope. The immortal elegy *In Memoriam* was written upon the death of his closest friend, Arthur Henry Hallam. The poet was in deep despair, but he wrote in the hope that he would be sustained by his faith in God. A memorable line from this poem speaks of the "mighty hopes that make us men." Hope is a force essential to life for both men and women.

The famous agnostic and freethinker, Robert G. Ingersoll, was the epitome of hopelessness when his brother died. He had spent years denying and even mocking God, but when he suffered bereavement he began to rethink his concept of God. All these years he had scorned the concept of a God with a long beard seated on a throne; now he knew he had to search for a more mature concept. He began when he stood at his brother's grave and said, "Life is a narrow veil between the cold and barren peaks of two eternities. We strive in vain to look beyond the heights. We cry aloud and the only answer is the echo of our wailing cry. From the voiceless lips of the unreplying dead there comes no word . . . but in the night of death, hope sees a star, and listening love can hear the rustle of a wing."

The last lines are captivating not only in their grandeur and poetic expression, but in the truth conveyed. Hope sees a star. Our hope gives us the vision to see in the night—even in the night of sorrow.

In the night of death, hope sees a star and listening love can hear the rustle of a wing. Will hope enable us to look up and see the light of God and the stars of holiness? Will listening love enable us to hear the still small voice of divinity speaking within our hearts, comforting us, summoning us not to weep for the departed, but to live for them?

EVEN WHEN HE IS SILENT

Toward the close of World War II, the Allied armies finally reached Cologne. Soldiers were assigned to make a house-to-house search for snipers or any high-ranking Nazis. Slowly, painstakingly, they made their way through the rubble of the destroyed city. Walking within the ruins of a large house, a soldier found a trapdoor leading to a deep cellar. He called several of his comrades, and holding their guns in readiness, they moved cautiously down the steps. In the murky gloom they saw only a few pieces of old dusty furniture.

Before turning to leave, one of the soldiers swung his flashlight around. There on the wall was some writing with a name below it. It was plain that some refugees had hidden in the cellar to escape death at the hands of the Nazis, but evidently they had been discovered and sent to the death camps.

The beam of the flashlight played on the last words of one of these doomed people, and this is what the soldiers read:

I believe in the sun even when it is not shining,
I believe in love even when feeling it not.
I believe in God even when He is silent.

Here, despite all the death and unspeakable brutality around him, a person had testified to his unshakeable belief and hope in God. He maintained hope in the future when there seemed to be no future left but the death camps of Europe. Maybe he too cried out of his despair, "Why, God, why? Why don't You answer? God, help us!" But he continued to believe in the sun, though living in the darkness of that cellar in Cologne. He continued to believe in love, though surrounded and threatened by hate. He continued to believe in God, even when He was silent.

According to the Jewish calendar, the day begins at sundown, not at sunrise. All festivals and holy days begin at night; the Sabbath begins at sundown. According to the Jewish tradition, this is of moral significance. It is easy to have confidence during the existence of sunlight. The Jewish day begins at night to symbolize that faith and hope will exist even in darkness, that light will prevail and that a new morrow will dawn upon all humankind.

Henry Ward Beecher once wrote of the "telescope of tears" to help us see beyond our sorrow. We need the telescope of faith to see beyond the darkness. We need hope to see a star and listening love to hear the rustle of a wing that heralds a new light and a new dawn.

We have cried, mourned, protested, and retreated deep within ourselves; we have been angry, anxious, and depressed. Now we have to ask ourselves what viable options are left open to us. We can think of committing suicide, mourning forever, or escaping to another part of the country or the world. Or we can get back into life with hope in the future, determined with self-management, knowing there is no alternative. We can say, "There's no use in trying. I'm through, finished with living." Or we can say, "No matter what, despite everything, I will go on and declare with the Psalmist, 'I will not die, but live.' "

WHAT YOU THINK—YOU ARE!

At times it may still seem that all hope is lost, that life is a covenant with sorrow and that there can never be joy, love, or a better tomorrow.

Jeremiah felt that way when the land was devastated and the Temple in ruins: "My heart within me is broken. All my bones shake." He then became determined to do something about his hopelessness. It was at this time that he bought land in Judea to show his hope in the days, months, and years that were yet to be. Even when his people were in exile and there seemed to be no hope, his faith strengthened him to hear, "Thus saith the Lord. Refrain thine voice from weeping and thine eyes from tears. . . . There is hope for thy future sayeth the Lord" (Jeremiah 31: 16–17).

Jeremiah thought hopeful thoughts and he became hopeful. What about your thoughts and feelings? What are you thinking? What you and I think determines how we feel, how we act, and what we are.

"You're not what you think you are, but what you think, you are." This was the opinion of William James (1842–1910), the American psychologist. He could have added, "You are not what you feel you are, but what you think, you feel." An ancient Greek philosopher said the same thing: "You feel what you think."

What was the greatest suffering you ever experienced? Was it physical, mental, or emotional? Most of us would answer "emotional." This is consistent with studies that indicate that the most severe, intense suffering human beings experience is due to emotional anguish rather than physical pain.

And yet, while we believe this suffering is caused by our emotions and feelings, in actuality it is caused by our thoughts. Agree or disagree? You are not what you think you are, but *what you think, you are!*

It is popular today to refer to feelings. "I feel that ... ," "It is my feeling that . . . ," "I have feelings of fear, frustration, and anxiety." It would be more accurate to state, "I think that . . . ," "It is my thought that . . . ," "I have thoughts of fear, frustration, and anxiety."

Our feelings come from our thoughts. We have thoughts of fear, guilt, shame, frustration, and grief; but we incorrectly believe we have those feelings. If we were able to go inside of ourselves and observe our feelings, we would not see any labels such as "guilt feeling," "fear feeling," or "grief feeling," but only unlabeled, miserable, and troubled feelings that are the result of our thoughts.

If William James and some of our contemporary psychologists are correct, then we all have been spending too much time examining and evaluating our feelings instead of our thoughts. What are you thinking? If you think thoughts of hopelessness, there is no hope. If you think thoughts of despair, there is only despair. If you think thoughts of joy and the coming of tomorrow, then you will turn yourself in the direction of the future.

Ralph Waldo Emerson once said, "A man is what he thinks about all day long."

Others who speak about positive and hopeful thinking are Norman Vincent Peale and Dale Carnegie, and what they teach is predicated on the psychological insight, "You are not what you think you are—but what you think, you are."

There is really nothing new about this belief. It had been stated in many different ways before William James, and many more after. What may be new is putting this idea to work for us here and now.

If we think of ourselves as failures, we are failures, and we feel failure. If we think of ourselves as inadequate, frustrated, unworthy, unloved, grieving human beings, that is exactly the way we will feel, and that is the way we will act. And through the self-fulfilling prophecy, that is the way we shall continue to be in the future.

THINK HOPEFULLY

If, however, we think of ourselves as hopeful and choosing, we will feel ourselves to be hopeful and choosing persons. If our thoughts determine our feelings, then we can make a start to think happy, think optimistic, and that is how we will feel. Consequently, we will be on the way to achieving a self-fulfilling prophecy that works for us instead of against us.

Remember William James and the saying, "You're not what you think you are, but what you think, you are." Start now by thinking positively and hopefully, "I am going to get well. I am going to get over my present feelings and thinking. I am going to get back to work and to life." Say yes to life, yes to hope, and you will be saying yes to yourself.

Once we decide to deal positively, optimistically, and hopefully with our thoughts and our feelings, we are on our way to a new and promising tomorrow.

Do you believe the Holy Scripture, "Weeping may tarry for the night but joy cometh in the morning"? Will you think about the possibility of joy coming in the morning? Will you think about the hope and promise of the future? Or is your mind so filled with thoughts of gloom and sadness that there isn't room for thoughts of renewed joy and hope? If this is so, it may not be the end but a portent of a new beginning. Fill your mind with thoughts of the happy times you had together with your loved one, the joy, the love you experienced together. Be optimistic with the thought that you will not always hurt this way. Concentrate on the positive, the hopeful prospects of tomorrow. Think hopefully and you will be hopeful.

There is a story of two mountain climbers who were ascending the Pyrenees:

One was a veteran and the other was a novice on his first climb. They climbed to a high mountain peak and rested for the night.

In what seemed to be the middle of the night, the novice was terrified at the howling of the wind, the thunder, and flashes of lightning. It seemed that the whole world was shaking and breaking into pieces. In his panic he cried out, "It's the end of the world. Everything is collapsing. There can never be a tomorrow again."

The veteran mountain climber soothed him, saying,

"No, it's not the end of everything. It's just the beginning. This is the way dawn comes to the Pyrenees."

Sometimes it's that way with us. Before the dawn of hope and fulfillment, we must first experience the night of weeping, loneliness, despair, and hopelessness.

It was Charles Beard who said, "When it's dark, look to the stars, and when it's too dark to see the stars, prepare to greet the dawn."

Confront your grief. Face it in all its dark and sorrowful reality. Then after facing it, you will know that there is no alternative—you must prepare to meet and greet the dawn of a new life and a new tomorrow.

I can almost hear you say, "You're right, I should do this. But how can I? What will force me, compel me to look at my grief and go on from there? Where can I find the faith that will motivate me to look through the darkness and the night to a new hope, a new light, and a new tomorrow filled with the beckoning possibilities of love, laughter, joy, and life?"

OUT OF DARKNESS AND THE SHADOW OF DEATH

An ancient parable tells that on the first day of Adam's life he saw the sun go down and was terrified.

> Darkness was beginning to envelop the world in its shadowy embrace. Paralyzed by fear and dread, Adam cried out, "God, where is the light? Is it gone forever? Will it ever come back again?"
>
> It was then that God gave him the intuition to take two stones, one called darkness and the other the shadow of death. Adam took the two stones and struck them together in frenzied desperation. He looked, and suddenly there were sparks, and there was light. Light had not been taken from his world forever.

Out of darkness and the shadow of death, there could still be the return of hope and light. Adam learned this. Have you?

To believe in God is to believe that He will not abandon us to a meaningless life and the absolute annihilation of death. When we feel that life makes no sense and death is an eternal zero, we turn to faith, which tells us that there is meaning in human existence.

What that meaning is we cannot know for certain, but this we believe, and we will shout it loud enough for the entire cosmos to hear: We care about human beings, human existence, and the human future. We have hope for humankind and believing this, we must have hope for tomorrow. There is no alternative. With hope we are inextricably bound to meaning. When we are in touch with meaning then we feel ourselves in touch with God. When we are in touch with God, we are standing at the doorway of meaning. Before we can reach out to God, our fellow human beings, and meaning, we must first reach into ourselves to find the hidden resources waiting to be found and used.

How can you find the strength and the will to hope again? Look within, the strength is within you. Pray to God to renew your faith in Him. Renew your hope, and at the same time, renew your life.

One Step at a Time!

Which makes more sense to you: "Where there's hope, there's life," or "Where there's life, there's hope"?

❧ ☙

Accept the life-sustaining power of hope.

❧ ☙

Think about the consequences of hopelessness and despair and then resolve to adopt an attitude of hope whether you feel like it or not.

❧ ☙

Turn to God to help you help yourself to hope again.

❧ ☙

If you are what you think, force yourself to reject negative thinking and allow only positive, hopeful thoughts to fill your mind.

7

When Fear Has Said Its Prayers

❧ ❧

Courage is fear that has said its prayers.
—Karle Wilson Baker

I T MAY BE DIFFICULT, but it is important that we alter and even revolutionize our thinking to regard death as "the ultimate friend." We know we are on the way to a developing maturity when we can think of death and say, "Even death can be good."

The story of Honi, the Rip Van Winkle of the Talmud, teaches us that death may be accepted as a blessing:

Once when Honi was worshipping and studying in the synagogue, he heard the sages teaching that everyone needs someone, and death may be welcomed as a friend. Honi scoffed at this, and left the synagogue thinking, "I am self-sufficient. I don't need anyone. As for death, my identity is with life and I will *never* welcome death as a friend or a blessing."

Musing about this teaching, he walked into a pasture nearby where an old man was planting a carob tree. Honi said to him, "Since a carob tree does not bear fruit

for seventy years, old man, you will never live long
enough to eat of its fruit."

The old man answered, "I found the world filled with
carob trees. As my forefathers planted them for me, I
likewise plant them for my descendants."

"Stupid old man," thought Honi, as he stretched out
and fell asleep. While he slumbered a grotto grew
around him so that he was hidden from view. And he
slept for seventy years.

On awakening, he was shocked to find he had grown
a long white beard. Beholding a man gathering carobs
from the tree, Honi asked him, "Do you know who
planted this carob tree?"

The man replied, "My grandfather."

Honi exclaimed, "Surely seventy years have passed
like a dream!"

Then he went to his house and inquired about the son
of Honi. He was told that his son was no more, but
Honi's grandson was living. He said to the people, "I am
Honi," but they called him a madman and drove him
away. Honi searched for his friends but they had died
or moved to other villages.

Feeling very much alone, he went to the synagogue
and heard the sages say, "It was seventy years ago today
that Honi disappeared."

He interrupted them saying, "I am Honi," but they
did not believe him. Lonely, tired, unhappy, without
friends or family, he thereupon prayed to God that he
might die. The Angel of Death came to him as a friend
and led him to eternal sleep.

THE GOD OF DEATH

In our grief, and especially when we feel ourselves
gripped by the fear of death—the death of dear ones,
or our own death—we should remember that God is
the God of death as well as of life. Death may be the
ultimate friend.

When we are young, death seems too horrible even to think about. It is so far away and remote that it does not seem real until someone we love dies. Then in our bereavement death dominates our feelings, our thoughts, and our lives. We shudder emotionally at the thought that this will happen to us, unaware that a time may come when we may feel differently, when we may even welcome death as a friend who releases us from the pain and the disabilities of life.

Death is becoming less of a taboo subject. Today the fields of medicine and psychology are joining religion in helping us to find the courage and support not only to face our fear of death, but to regard death as an ultimate good. In recent years thanatology, the study of death, has almost become a subspecialty of psychology, psychiatry, nursing, and the social sciences. To date, some seventy American colleges and schools offer courses on thanatology. Three journals are currently published which specifically deal with issues of death and dying.

There are at least two institutions specializing in the study of death. One is the Center for Death Education and Research located in the Department of Sociology at the University of Minnesota. The other is the Center for Psychological Studies of Dying, Death, and Lethal Behavior at Wayne State University in Detroit. In addition, other research is being carried on in a number of universities and hospitals in the United States and Europe.

Early in the 1960s, Dr. Eric Kast found that psychedelic drugs, particularly LSD, helped patients to find relief from their fear of death and even to anticipate death as something beautiful, welcome, and sublime.

At the Maryland Psychiatric Center in Catonsville scientists are experimenting with psychedelic drugs to ease the transition from life to death and to bring relief, tranquility, and acceptance to the dying. The patients take a psychedelic trip through the valley of the shadow of death and return with a more composed and accepting attitude toward death. This is only a portent of some of the experiments and research projects that are being pursued in an effort to meet the needs of the dying.

While research scientists attempt to find ways for us to face our fear of death and the anguish of bereavement, we have to start now to take steps of our own to lead us into new avenues of living.

In her own pioneering studies of death, Dr. Elisabeth Kübler-Ross of the University of Chicago has discovered that those who face death usually go through five stages: denial, anger, negotiation, depression, and acceptance.

The living who face the fear of death in their bereavement go through some of the same stages. We, too, experience our own denial, anger, and depression. It is too late for us to negotiate now. We tried to make deals with God for more time while our dear ones were dying. Now we can achieve acceptance by yielding with the resignation of faith to the reality of the death of our dear ones and of ourselves. What will strengthen us for acceptance?

EXCESSIVE GRIEF AND DEPRESSION

We are here now. Despite our sorrow we want to live. Yet excessive grief and depression may bring about the very thing we try so scrupulously to avoid— our own death. This does not mean that we should not grieve or mourn. It does mean that extreme and prolonged grief may hurt or even kill us.

Are we helping those for whom we mourn? Are we changing anything by delaying our recovery from grief? Will all our tears bring the dead back to us? Will our sorrow help them to live again?

It is good to give expression to our feelings, and it is helpful to express our deep and painful bereavement. There must come a time, however, when we stop to consider what we are doing to ourselves through our continued agony and uneasing torment.

Dr. Martin Seligman, a psychologist at the University of Pennsylvania, believes that "human beings die following experiences of helplessness." This may sound extreme, but his studies show that the death of a loved one may lead to the premature death of the mourner.

The death of loved ones may induce thoughts of suicide. We want to escape from our pain; we want to blot out our memory and sink into total oblivion. Our anger causes us to rage against life and against God. Fear and hostility are sometimes expressed by self-inflicted injuries. The fear represents hostility that is projected outward and the injuries of hostility are turned inward.

Seligman recommends that anyone who is already weakened by physical sickness or mental depression should have a medical checkup when a major psychological stress occurs, particularly bereavement. Dr. Erich Lindemann discloses that there is a correlation between asthma, rheumatoid arthritis, and ulcerative colitis in cases of excessive and continued grieving.

You do not need psychological research to convince you what depression, grief, and excruciating mental anguish can do to you emotionally and physically. You know how miserable you feel. You know how much you hurt. You may not know, however, that unless you work through your grief, your fears, and your stress, you are doing what may be irreversible damage to your heart, cardiovascular and gastrointestinal systems, your blood pressure, and the entire network of your nervous system.

There are some who punish themselves by punishing other people. Through this self-chastisement they may hurt other members of their family, as though they hold them responsible for the tragedy. They resent members of the family and friends who are trying to make their way back to life again.

There are also those who are determined to dull the edge of all feeling. With excessive and protracted grief, some try to escape through alcohol, only to find themselves trapped in another world of artificial well-being, an externally induced tranquility that allows them to forget the pain for a while. As a consequence they become accomplices to their own destruction, causing irreparable damage not only to their kidneys, liver, pancreas, and stomach, but also causing permanent impairment of the brain.

Some try to escape from the reality of grief by seeking the forgetfulness of sleep. They may take tranquilizers and sleeping pills to blot out the world of reality.

All this constitutes the fulfillment of a subconscious wish to commit suicide. It is not entirely accidental that so many who experience bereavement and grief are involved in serious traffic accidents. It is not entirely coincidental that so many in grief try to join their dear ones by "accidentally" drowning or by slipping, falling, and hurting themselves in household "accidents."

Is this the kind of tribute you want to pay to those who loved you? Is this evidence of your gratitude to those you still love? Are you such a masochist or martyr that you want to hurt yourself for those who always brought you healing? Do you want the thought that you love them with all your heart to mean that you sacrifice the healthy functioning of your heart because of their death? Will your willingness to give your life for them come literally true? Is this the kind of futility they would want for you? Would they want you to die for them, or live for them by dedicating your life to the ideals and values that were so important, valued, and meaningful to them? Only you can answer these questions.

A WORK OF GREAT MERCY

At a time of great anguish, Eli Melech, a sage of ancient times, brooded in his grief. His dead teacher appeared to him. Eli Melech cried out, "Why are you silent in such dreadful need?" His teacher answered, "In heaven we see that all that seems evil to you is a work of mercy." Could it be true of our dead, too? Could it be that what seems evil to us is really a work of mercy?

In the Book of the Wisdom of Solomon we read these words of comfort: "The souls of the righteous are in the hands of God and no evil shall touch them. In the eyes of men they seem to have died, and their departure is accounted to be their hurt. But they are at peace."

But what about us? We meditate on these words as we think tenderly and lovingly of those who have been summoned from this earth to life everlasting with God. We remember when they walked among us in the land of the living, their love answering to ours, their hands reaching out to ours, and their hearts responding to ours. We yearn for comfort, consolation, and peace because their visible presence is with us no more. We lift our eyes on high; we elevate our vision above our sorrow, and we know that in the night of death, hope sees a star.

Through faith we gain the acuity of vision to see a star, even in the night of sorrow, and know that our dear ones are with God.

Through faith we gain that listening love that enables us to hear our dear ones speaking to us, saying, "Even though you cannot understand, grief is experienced only by the living. Pain is the heritage of mortality. Even though our departure is accounted to be our hurt, we are at peace. We are with God. Our destiny is with infinite love."

As grief is experienced only by the living, so fear is experienced only by the living. We believe that fear is never experienced by the dead, and seldom by the dying.

The poet, Walter Savage Landor, believed that

Death stands above me, whispering low
I know not what into my ear;
Of his strange language all I know
Is, there is not a word of fear.*

This I believe. In my experience of over forty years in dealing with death, I have heard people express fear some time before their death, but seldom have I ever seen someone afraid when death was very near. It is as if God had placed a sedative in the bloodstream. The life processes slow down and the dying feel weary. There is a yearning to sleep, quietly and undisturbed. There is the calm and serenity of acceptance, almost as if they were saying,

---

* From *A Treasury of Comfort,* edited by Sidney Greenberg (Hartmore House, 1954). Copyright 1954 by Sidney Greenberg. Reprinted by permission of the editor.

Yea, though I walk through the valley of the shadow of death, I will fear no evil, for Thou art with me. . . .

Dr. Frank Adair, who studied the subject of death for many years, wrote that "the haunting fear which the average person carries all through life is dissipated by the approach of death." We worry unduly most of our lives about a fear that we will never experience—not only the fear of death, but the fear of dying.

W. H. Auden must have known this because when the time came when he was about to die, he said, "Thank you, fog. Sleep, big baby, sleep your fill."

No Alternative

We must confront without fear the reality of the death of our loved ones and our own death. We can live for them or die for them. We can maintain a continued hurt or find a creative healing. When we once considered their dying, there was no alternative; and now that they are dead, what alternatives do we have?

When the infant state of Israel was born, and the Israelis were attacked by powerful adversaries and were hopelessly outnumbered, they utilized what they have since called their most effective weapon—their motto, *"Ayn Berayra"*—"No Alternative"). They had to be victorious to survive. The alternative to victory was annihilation and being driven into the sea.

This must be our motto, too. No alternative!

We have to face our fear of death and go on living. No alternative! We have no choice but to restructure our thoughts and our lives, knowing that though the wound of bereavement will heal, there will always be a scar. No alternative! We must pay tribute to our dead, not by testimonials of tears or monuments of grief, but by allowing the memory of love to lead us to love even more, by allowing the memory of giving to motivate us to give even more, and by allowing the memory of their service to others to inspire us to serve others even more.

How many times have you said, "I wanted you to live —only to live. Just to know that I can see you again, to watch you smile through your pain—but to know that you are"? But do you have an alternative?

Suppose our beloved had lived and we had watched them gradually lose the dignity of body and mind? Is this what they would have wanted? Would we have wanted them to suffer with no release from pain? We wanted to hold onto them and never let them go. We cried. We prayed. We pleaded that they live. But the time for eternal rest had come. No alternative exists but to face our fear of death with courage and faith.

If I knew of a drug or medicine that would alleviate the pain of grief experienced by the living, would I not rush to tell you about it? LSD may be used for the terminally ill, but what about so many of us who are experiencing bereavement? There is something other than drugs that can help us. There is something we can use to ease our pain and help us to live again, and that is a meaningful religious faith.

COURAGE IS FEAR THAT HAS SAID ITS PRAYERS

Karle Wilson Baker was looking right at us when she wrote,

Courage is armour
A blind man wears;
The calloused scars

Of out-lived despairs;
Courage is fear
That has said its prayers.*

This is true for us, too. Confronted by a myriad of doubts, apprehensions, anxieties, and fears, we need the courage that is engendered by a fear that has said its prayers. Professor Alfred North Whitehead was correct when he said that it is through the facing of fear and dread that man truly arrives at a religious faith that is founded on the love of God.

Abraham, Isaac, Jacob, and Jesus, the patriarchs, prophets, and sages all experienced fear, but through their fear they found the way to God. Moses was afraid, but his fear said its prayers, and then "Moses drew near unto the thick darkness where God was." A religious faith helps us to find the armor of courage to meet the challenge of life after we face our fear of death. A religious faith gives us the assurance that we are not alone—God is with us even in the thick darkness of the soul.

Death should be looked upon as an inevitable consequence of life, but even more, as a natural and essential part of God's plan and design for man. If so, why should we fear death?

No, we should not fear death, but what if we do? Then we need support and faith to strengthen and gird us in our fears. People love the Twenty-third Psalm. You may find other psalms that are more beautiful and more exalted. But why does this one have such a universal appeal? Because, "Though I walk through the valley of the shadow of death, I will fear no evil." Why?

* "Courage," by Karle Wilson Baker, in *Dreams on Horseback* (Southwest Press, n.d.). Reprinted by permission of the Estate of Karle Wilson Baker.

"For Thou art with me." It is the presence of God that allows our fear to say its prayers.

We do not say with Auden, "Thank you, Fog." We do not say with Browning, "To feel the fog in my throat, the mist in my face, the power of the night, the press of the storm, the post of the foe, there he stands, the arch fear in visible form," but we ask in the language of faith,

> Help us to understand, O Lord, that grief and love go hand in hand, that the sorrow of loss is but a token of the love that is stronger than death. Even though we cry in the bereavement of our hearts when our beloved are taken from this earth, may it be as a child cries who knows his father is near, who clings unafraid to a trusted hand. In this spirit, O Thou who art the Master of our destiny, do we commit all that is precious to us into Thy keeping, knowing that death is not the end. The earthly body vanishes; the immortal spirit lives on with God. In our hearts, also, our loved ones never die. Their love and memory abide as a lasting inspiration moving us to noble deeds and blessing us evermore.

C. S. Lewis, who called upon God in vain, allowed his fear to say its prayers, and then he wrote, "And so, perhaps with God. I have gradually been coming to feel that the door was no longer shut and bolted. Was it my own frantic need that slammed it in my face?"

His diary ends with a reconciliation. He interprets this as evidence that the dead may survive as "pure intelligence"—at once their essential selves and an aspect of God—and this helps him to reestablish the continuity of life.

Following the death of a dear one, novelist Emily Brontë allowed her fear to say its prayers as she said,

No coward soul is mine,
No trembler in the world's storm-troubled sphere.
I see Heaven's glories shine,
And faith shines equal, arming me from fear. . . .

There is not room for Death,
Nor atom that His might could render void;
Thou—Thou art Being and Breath,
And what Thou art may never be destroyed.

To believe in God, not because of proof, and not because of miracles, is to believe in the divinity of human beings, the eternalness of the human soul, and the immortality that showers the night with stars.

When fear has said its prayers, we are helped to find a living faith. With such a living faith do we find comfort, consolation, and peace as we let our grief and our sorrow help us to find ways to a new life, to new living, and especially to new loving. Then we will know a healing sorrow that will send us forth to serve and bless the living. We will know that the loveliness that dies when we forget, comes alive when we remember.

One Step at a Time!

Take a moment or two to think about the possibility of death being a friend.

⋅≼ ≽⋅

Decide to cope with your grief because excessive grief is damaging to your physical, emotional, and mental health.

⋅≼ ≽⋅

Understand that darkness is the prelude to the dawn.

⋅≼ ≽⋅

Let your prayers reinforce your belief that where there's hope, there's life, and there is hope for a happier tomorrow.

⋅≼ ≽⋅

You have tried everything else; try turning to God for help, strength, and hope.

8

The Daring Dream

❧ ❧

*What a wonder it is—the great fact, or hope,
or daring dream of immortality.*
    —William Pierson Merrill

T HE QUESTION OF WHETHER there is life after death
has been examined and debated ever since the
dawn of human history. The mind rebels at the very
thought of the oblivion of one's self, the extinction of
the ego. We want to live. We want our loved ones to
live. We want to continue to live after the brief number
of years on this earth. We want to believe that there is
something more.

The span of human life is so brief, like the shadow of
a bird in flight. Is that all? Whatever that life is in the
next world, we want it. We want eternal life.

Fearing the extinction of self and the end of life,
humankind has attempted to assuage the shock of
death through the promise of a continued existence.
The ancient Hebrews wrote about Sheol, Gehinom,
and Pardes (Paradise). The Christian tradition antici-
pates the promise of heaven. The ancient Greeks spoke

of a paradisiacal existence in the Elysian Fields, the Hindus believed in Nirvana, the Scandinavians held out the prospect of Valhalla, the Persians spoke of an Abode of Song, and the American Indian sought to pass on to the Happy Hunting Ground.

Countless millions have clung tenaciously to the hope of eternal life beyond the grave. This hope, born out of the "will to live," has caused them to be theologically seduced by the alluring promise of a heavenly bliss beyond all human understanding. This hope has caused them to be terrorized by the ominous threat of eternal hell and damnation. Like a shiny new toy, the promise of heaven has been held before man as an inducement for being good. The consequences of disobedience and sin are measured by a divine bogeyman as a deferred payment in an afterlife of eternal punishment in hell. Such childlike eagerness for reward and the infantile dread of punishment have been exploited by medicine men, shamans, religious functionaries, and ecclesiastical bodies for the purpose of securing absolute commitment and unquestioning obedience.

We grasp at every straw of credence that will sustain the possibility of some kind of immortality. What else can we believe? That we have our brief span of existence on earth, and then we and those we love are no more?

It is not enough for most of us to believe that dust returns to dust. We need to believe that the spirit returns to the God who created it, that the soul is transmuted to everlasting sleep or eternal life with God. Those who are bereaved cry out, "I want to see them again. I want to see more than a soul—I want to see my dear one again in person. I don't want a vague, spiritual, ethereal reunion of souls. When I die I want to live

again, not just as a blob of energy or as a memory. To
live on in someone's memory isn't enough. To live on
through my deeds isn't enough. I want to continue to
be me. I want to be."

It is presumptuous for any mortal human being to
attempt to define what happens after death. It is difficult enough to comprehend what is happening in this
life. There are so many questions. Does the soul have
consciousness, awareness? Will there be feeling, cognition, knowledge of one's own being, of other beings? Or
will the soul be merged with the universal, eternal mystery—the soul of God, with no ego identification, no
selfhood? This is the fear of the void, the terror of nothingness that comes to all of us.

To face our apprehension about the mystery of life
beyond the grave, we need not the blind, unthinking
acceptance of the beast of the field, nor resignation, but
the questioning, constructive faith which makes life
livable and robs death of its terror.

When a person dies, we can observe the disintegration of the body. However, no disintegration of the
spiritual self is observable. We make a covenant with a
mystery and take the leap of faith that allows us to
believe that the spiritual self partakes of the nature of
God and that the image of God is not subject to disintegration or decay.

It is on the basis of such considerations that most
religions affirm that death is not the end, that God has
implanted eternal life within us. We have no certain
way of knowing exactly what is going to happen to us
after we die.

Elisabeth Kübler-Ross of the University of Chicago,
physician, psychiatrist, and scientist, believes in life
after death. Why shouldn't we? But reason intrudes to

remind us that dust returns to dust. How can there be intelligence without a brain? How can there be cognition, feeling, and emotion without a mind and a heart, without the chemistry that enables us to laugh, cry, and experience being human? Is the hope for immortality only a yearning for wish fulfillment? Is it a daring dream?

THE GREAT PERHAPS

While there can be no strong faith without doubts, there comes a time when we should begin to reassess our doubts. When we doubt the worth and sanctity of life, when we doubt ethical and moral values, the integrity of our fellow man, the existence of God, and the hope of immortality, we might consider "The Great Perhaps."

Consider that most patients do not have to be told when they are terminally ill. They seem to know. The doctor may refuse to acknowledge it, the family may deny it, but I have heard many patients say, "Even though I believe it's hopeless, maybe, perhaps—perhaps I'm wrong." They lapse into a blessed coma with comfort, with hope—never sure, but always considering The Great Perhaps.

The nineteenth century poet John Neihardt called the afterlife "The Grey Perhaps." Thornton Wilder refers to immortality, the postulate of life after death, as "The *Great* Perhaps." There are many who cannot quite believe in an existence in the next world, or a life after death, that is, a conscious life. But there are times when we doubt our doubts and say, "Perhaps I'm wrong. Perhaps there *is* something. No one really knows."

The Great Perhaps may apply to our doubts about the existence of God.

An atheist went to visit a clergyman to debate whether or not God existed. When the teacher came into the room, he looked at the atheist and said, "I will not debate with you, or give you arguments and reasons for the existence of God. Just ask yourself one word: 'Perhaps—perhaps.' " The atheist was struck dumb, too frightened and shaken to even speak.

Could this apply to our hopes and doubts about immortality, too? Our hope for immortality surges up in a poem, a picture, the sound of music, whispering the belief that life does not end with the breath, that death is not just a door out of life, but a door that leads into a new life.

A wise teacher once taught, "In all the time that I spend arguing about God, or defining His attributes, His Being, in all the time I spend arguing about immortality or defining immortality, I could be stringing pearls for the sake of heaven. Each pearl is a good deed, an act of kindness, an act of compassion, an act of love to be strung on a heavenly necklace. Talk about God, pray to God, say 'Perhaps,' but above all attest to God through your deeds of compassion and loving kindness."

It is well that we consider this when in moments of doubt we ask ourselves, "Does God really hear prayer?" *Perhaps.* When we doubt and ask ourselves, "Does God really know my actions, my thoughts, see my every deed?" *Perhaps.* "Is there a God who cares about me in my sorrow, a God who is concerned about what I do, the way I treat my fellow man, my justice or lack of it, my compassion or lack of it?" *Perhaps.* "Is there really a life after death?" *Perhaps.*

Then let all the maybes and all the perhapses motivate and lead us, not only to think and question, but to act in such a way that we string pearls of kindness, compassion, and love for the sake of our departed dear ones, for God's sake, and for our own sake.

THE DARING DREAM

What if there is a life after death? What kind of life is it? Can any mortal being answer this question? Scripture teaches us that "the secret things belong to God, but the things that are revealed belong unto us" (Deut. 29:29). How can we learn of the unknowable mysteries of eternity when we have not yet discovered the meaning of the knowable mysteries of life on earth?

Neither science nor religion can determine or prove the nature of life beyond the grave. In the effort to arrive at conclusions, hypotheses, and beliefs, religion uses the term "faith." But science uses the term "statistical probabilities." Science requires empirical knowledge and demonstrable proof. What proof is there that there will be a tomorrow? There is none, and therefore "tomorrow" cannot be a scientific reality subject to validation. Science adheres to the belief in a tomorrow because of statistical probabilities. Religion calls it faith.

Many scientists are either dubious or agnostic about the unknown. With growing interest in psychic phenomena, extra-sensory perception, and the infinite possibilities of psychic energy, some scientists are beginning to take a new look at The Great Perhaps. Philosophers, psychologists, and scholars are reconsidering the possibilities of what William Pierson Merrill called the "hope or daring dream of immortality."

Man may never know with certainty what awaits him after death. But as he searches for answers, the hope for immortality is in his mind or hidden in his heart.

I once went into a mortuary to pay my respects to the memory of a dear friend. As I waited for the family, a woman walked up to me and asked me if I would go with her to another room to see "something beautiful."

I walked with her to the other room and saw an open coffin. In it was the body of an eight-year-old girl with golden curly hair. The woman said, "That's my daughter. Isn't she beautiful!"

"Yes," I replied.

The woman said, "I am so happy. She is now in heaven, with wings. And when I die, she will come out to meet me. I will first hold her in my arms and embrace her. And then, do you know what I'm going to do next? I'm going to wash her hair and put it up in golden curls as I've always done. Won't that be beautiful?"

As I returned to the other room to await the family, I thought, "What wonderful faith. I wish I could believe as she believes." However, my reason will not let me. How can I believe that a child will rush to meet her mother and that they will embrace in another world? How can I believe that the mother will wash her child's hair and set it in golden curls as she had always done? I just could not and I still cannot, because of my belief that dust returns to dust and the spirit returns to God who gave it.

Had I said to the bereaved mother that I did not believe her daughter would have a body in the next world, but an immortal soul, she might have been disillusioned, hurt, and even crushed. I can hear her say, "I don't want to hug a disembodied spirit. I don't want to put my arms around a soul. I want to put my arms around my darling daughter—to touch her, feel her warmth, and kiss her again."

The woman had indicated that she believed her child would have a spiritual body. At first thought, that seemed a contradiction in terms until I pondered the

teachings of Albert Einstein and learned that everything is matter and can be converted into other forms
of matter. There is nothing more firmly established in
science than the laws of conservation of matter and of
force. No single atom in creation can cease to exist, it
can only change in form. We cannot burn up anything
into nothingness, we can only change it from a solid to
a gaseous state. Neither is any energy or force ever
destroyed, it is only changed from one form to another,
steam into electricity and electricity into light or music
or X-rays. If this principle is true of matter and force,
is it not likely to be true of that form or force which we
call life?

It could be that Norman Cousins is right when he
declares in "Celebration of Life" that "my substance is
boundless and infinite. The portion of that substance
that is mine was not devised; it was renewed. So long
as the human bloodstream lives I have life. Of this does
my immortality consist. . . . We are single cells in a body
of three billion cells. The body is humankind."

DOES THE SOUL LIVE FOREVER?

You may be thinking, "Who cares whether Norman
Cousins is right or wrong. I'm not interested in that
kind of immortality—to be a part of the human bloodstream, or cells in a body of three billion cells. I'm not
interested in being a part of infinity, or of merging my
soul with the universal, cosmic soul. Words! Words! I
want to feel that there is something about my dear ones
that continues to live. Don't tell me that he or she lives
in my memory; I want more than memory. I want them
to live, and I want to live! Forget this ersatz, this hypo-
thetical verbiage. Is there a soul? Does the soul live?
What kind of life does it live?"

Is the hope of immortality a daring dream? Is it The Great Perhaps? Or is it a theological lie perpetuated by religious con artists to delude the naive, and exploit the hopes and fears of the gullible who want to buy a commodity that does not exist?

Some of us maintain an unquestioning belief in immortality. Others believe that the body disintegrates completely and there is no extension of consciousness, ego, or form, and no possibility of immortality beyond the grave.

Could it be that there is truth somewhere between the two extremes? There is one belief of Ecclesiastes that "for to him that is joined to all the living there is hope; for a living dog is better than a dead lion. For the living know that they shall die; but the dead know not any thing, neither have they any more a reward; for the memory of them is forgotten. As well their love, as their hatred and their envy, is long ago perished; neither have they any more a portion forever in anything that is done under the sun" (Ecc. 9:4–6).

There is the belief of Rabelais: "Ring the curtain down; the farce is over. If a man die, does he desire to live again? What has my life meant to anyone?" And there is the belief of Isaiah and the teachers of the New Testament that "thy dead shall live again."

Could it be that despite all our emphasis on energy and psychic research, our mortal, rational, pseudo-scientific thinking has obscured the possibility of immortality and life after death?

THE CANDLE DOES NOT GO OUT

When Sir Arthur Keith, one of the great British scientists, stated that at death a man goes out like a candle, Professor Arthur H. Compton replied that the candle does not go out; its energy goes on and on to the farthest reaches of the universe.

Many other scientists agree with this view. Professor Ashley Montague cites the law of conservation of energy, the idea that energy is neither created nor destroyed, as evidence of scientific belief in the imperishability of life. The indestructibility of matter and energy surely points to a kind of immortality.

THE OPENING OF ANOTHER DOOR

A sage who was about to die saw tears on the faces of his disciples and he asked, "Why do you cry? I'm leaving by one door only to enter by another."

When we begin life it is stretched before us like a corridor with many doors. We open and close the doors of infancy, adolescence, maturity, and old age. As we walk down the corridor, the doors close behind us one by one, year by year. We finally open the door for death and, as we do, we open yet another door for eternal life.

There are so many doors we never touch, and never open. Before it is too late, let us open the doors that lead to truth, comfort in our sorrow, and faith in immortality. More than anything else, let us open the doors to those things in life which abide eternally, those that give life meaning—the doors of tenderness and love.

It is not too late to love and it is not too late to live. It is not too late to thaw ourselves out of our chilling sorrow for the opportunities of living. It is not too late for those who are frozen by the coldness of grief, whose hearts have been made icy and unfeeling, to be warmed by giving life, hope, and love to others.

When we are exhausted, when we cannot go on anymore, taking the hand of someone who is weaker than we are gives us strength. When death closes the door to a life we have loved, it is futile to spend the rest of our days trying to batter down the door, or ask the unanswerable question: "Why did the door have to swing shut on me?" And it is a betrayal of our future to pretend that the door was never closed at all.

In the *N'eilah* Service during the Jewish Day of Atonement, there is a brief but beautiful prayer: "Open to us a gate at the time when a gate is closed." The author of the prayer was emphasizing a basic truth of life—God never closes a door in our lives without opening another.

Let our grief send us forth to serve and bless the living. Let our grief and our sorrow motivate us to greater compassion towards others. Let our grief and sorrow help us to open doors to new hope, to new life, to new living and especially, to new loving. Even in the darkness of our sorrow, we see the stars again when we bless and serve the living.

A PARABLE OF BIRTH

A contemporary Israeli rabbi, the late Rabbi Y. Tuckachinsky, asks us to imagine twins growing peacefully in the warmth of the womb.

> Their mouths are closed, and they are being fed via the navel. Their lives are serene. The whole world to these brothers is in the interior of the womb. Who could conceive anything larger, better, more comfortable?
>
> Then they begin to wonder, "We are moving lower and lower. Surely if it continues, we will exit one day. What will happen after we exit?"
>
> The first infant is a believer. He is heir to a religious tradition which tells him that there will be a "new life" after this wet and warm existence of the womb. It is a strange belief, seemingly without foundation, but one

to which he holds fast. The second infant is a true skeptic. Mere stories do not deceive him; he believes only in that which can be demonstrated. What is not within one's experience can have no basis in one's imagination.

Says the faithful brother, "After our 'death' here, there will be a great new world. We will eat through the mouth. We will see great distances, and we will hear through the ears on the sides of our heads. Why, our feet will be straightened! And our heads will be up and free, rather than down and boxed in."

Replies the skeptic, "Nonsense. You're straining your imagination again. There is no foundation for this belief. It is only your survival instinct, an elaborate defense mechanism, a historically conditioned subterfuge. You are looking for something to calm your fear of 'death.' There is only this world. There is no world to come!"

"Well, then," asks the first, "what do you say it will be like?"

The second brother snappily replies with all the assurance of the slightly knowledgeable, "We will go with a bang. Our world will collapse and we will sink into oblivion. No more. Nothing. Black void. An end to consciousness. Forgotten. This may not be a comforting thought, but it is a logical one."

Suddenly the water inside the womb bursts. The womb convulses. Upheaval. Turmoil. Everything lets loose. Then a mysterious pounding—a crushing, staccato pounding. Faster, faster, lower, lower.

The believing brother exits. Tearing himself from the womb, he falls outward. The second brother shrieks, startled by the "accident" befallen his brother. He bewails and bemoans the tragedy, the death of a perfectly fine fellow. Why? Why? Why didn't he take better care? Why did he fall into that terrible abyss?

As he thus laments, he hears a headsplitting cry, a

great tumult from the black abyss, and he trembles, "Oh my! What a horrible end! As I predicted!"

Meanwhile, as the skeptic brother mourns, his "dead" brother has been born into the "new" world. The head-splitting cry is a sign of health and vigor, and the tumult is really a chorus of "Mazel Tovs" (congratulations), sounded by the waiting family thanking God for the birth of a healthy son.

Indeed, in the words of a contemporary thinker, man comes from the darkness of the "not yet," and proceeds to the darkness of the "no more."

As we separate and "die" from the womb, only to be born to life, so we separate and die from our world, only to be reborn to life eternal. The exit from the womb is the birth of the body. The exit from the body is the birth of the soul. As the womb requires a gestation period of nine months, the world requires a residence of a certain number of years. As the womb is an ante-room preparatory to life, so our present existence is a vestibule to the world beyond.

DEATH IS NOT THE END

In the spiritual dimension of faith there is no death, only life on earth and life everlasting with God. We believe that death is not the end, but a new beginning. The earthly body vanishes, the immortal spirit lives on with God.

There is a beautiful prayer which says, "The soul which Thou, O God, hast given unto me came pure from Thee. Thou hast created it, Thou hast formed it, Thou hast breathed it into me. Thou hast preserved it in this body and, at the appointed time, Thou wilt take it from this earth that it may enter upon life everlasting."(Union Prayerbook, CCAR).

There is no fear, no apprehension, no dread of punishment in an afterworld. The soul which came from God returns to God. Can there be a greater good than to return to God, to be one with God? We cannot know. We cannot presume to comprehend the mystery of the unknown, but this we believe with perfect faith: That God is love, and there can be no greater good than returning to the source of universal love. That is why we repeat in the words of an ancient prayer,

> Into thy hands, O God, I commit my soul.
> And with my soul, my body, too.
> Both when I wake and when I sleep
> The Lord is with me, I shall not fear.

Do we fear the unknown for ourselves and for our dear ones? "I shall not fear." When a noted astronomer was dying, he was asked if he feared to go out into the unknown. He calmly replied, "I have loved the stars too fondly to be fearful of the night."

This is the essence of the daring dream: to believe in the immortality of the soul and in eternal life with God, but to make the love of God and humankind such a factor in our lives that we do not need an afterlife to recognize that our immortality is within us and yet transcends us, partaking of the past, present, and future. In order to learn how to die, we have to learn how to live, to live meaningfully and religiously with God-like values. The more holiness, justice, mercy, and love we bring into our lives and into our world, the more we assure ourselves of the sacred possibilities of the daring dream.

One Step at a Time!

Consider the belief in immortality—"The Great
Perhaps."

❧ ❧

Think about the possibility that there is more than
one reality.

❧ ❧

Say goodbye to the mortal existence of the departed,
and contemplate the mystery of a new beginning.

❧ ❧

Concentrate on the conviction that nothing that is of
God can ever really die.

❧ ❧

Maintain the faith that we move from life to life.

9

Where Death Can Serve
the Living
꿍커 여외

> *. . . not unavailing will be our grief if*
> *it sends us back to serve and bless . . . the*
> *living.*
> —Union Prayerbook (CCAR)

THE INSCRIPTION ABOVE THE doorway of the Sor-
bonne Medical School reads: "Here is where death
is made to serve the living." This statement could
mean something to us, that we too must find ways
that will permit our sorrow and grief to serve the
living.

We have cried our tears. We have dealt with our
grief. We are ready to make our covenant with life
again. Did we gain any wisdom from our bereavement?
Does our grief help us to go forth with compassion and
greater empathy to serve the living?

We have the opportunity to offer our departed dear
ones more than testimonials of tears and monuments of
grief. We can do more than cry for them. We can live
for them and the ideals, principles, and values they
cherished most. We can make of their memory a living
beacon that shows us the way to kindness and a sensitivity to the hurts and needs of others.

This may have been what Thomas Jefferson meant when he wrote to his friend James Madison, "Take care of me when I am dead." There is a deeper meaning to Jefferson's statement than a request for proper burial. Perhaps Jefferson was thinking of his unfinished work, the tasks of democracy that were yet to be completed. He was hoping that his friends and followers would take care of this work for him after his death.

Can't we hear our dear ones pleading for us to take care of some of their unfinished work, the tasks that were left incomplete? We have work to do. We can help to carry out their ideals and principles by getting outside of ourselves—by not only mourning for them, but working for them, loving for them, and living for them.

THE UNFINISHED AGENDA OF LOVE

We are part of our loved ones' unfinished agenda of love. They had so many hopes for us. How they longed to witness the fulfillment of our continuing maturity, the achievement of our ambitions and goals, and the realization of our dreams. They wanted to rejoice in the actualization of our potential for joy, happiness, service to others, and the zest for life. More than anything else, they yearned to be here to know that we love and are loved.

Are you doing anything about their unfinished hopes, dreams, and aspirations for you? If you have surrendered to defeatism, yielded to pessimism, and made a covenant with continuing sorrow and bereavement, you are not rendering a service but a disservice to the dead.

A televised documentary on the horrors of the Nazi concentration camps portrayed a man named Bach, who for thirty-five years after his release searched for his beloved friend. When at last Bach found him, he saw that his friend's mind was blank; he just was not the same person. So Bach went to his clergyman and asked whether it was permitted to say memorial prayers for his friend, even though he was still alive and breathing. His friend had died, even though his body still lived. Permission was granted.

Some of us die a long time before we stop breathing. We have no more promises to keep, no more people to love, and no more miles to go. We refuse to allow death to serve the living.

Even those who believe in life after death sometimes do not believe in life after death. No, the repetition is not a printer's error. It means that some of us do not believe in our own lives after the death of a dear one. Life can be lost without tomorrows. Life can be lost without love. Life can be lost without dreams, faith, and hope. But life can never be lost by another's death.

The great English statesman, Edmund Burke, was heartbroken by the death of his adored son. His soul was darkened. He knew despair as he dragged on day after day. But he knew something more. He knew that if he were to fulfill himself, he would have to work through his grief. That is why he adopted the motto "Work on."

We have work to do in our mourning. We have to live not only for ourselves, but for our loved ones, too—to follow in their ways, to work at their unfinished tasks, and to realize their unfinished dreams. We can do this only by living.

Turn Again to Life

Our dead live through us, through our deeds, through our actions. When we carry on their unfinished work and devote ourselves to brotherhood, our dead live. When we struggle for true democracy, implementing the values and the ideals of our democratic philosophy of government, our dead live. When we consecrate ourselves to freedom and dedicate ourselves to peace, then we know with compelling certainty that they have not departed from us, that they have not been turned from the realm of the living.

The thought of working on the unfinished hopes and dreams of our departed compels us to do some deep soul-searching about ourselves and the measure, worth, and meaning of our own lives.

> A man who continued to grieve for his wife and was unable to put himself together to return to the world of the living once cried out to a friend, "If only I could see her again—at this very moment!"
>
> His friend gently asked, "What if she were able to see *you* again, at this very moment?"
>
> The sorrowing husband said, "Oh, no! I wouldn't want her to see me the way I am now, unshaven, despairing, neglecting the children, not going back to work. I couldn't stand to have her see me this way!"

What if our dead could return? Would they be proud of us? Would they be pleased with what has happened to us? Would they think that their life and death helped us to live better lives, to achieve higher standards? Or would they think that the influence of their life and death had been completely inconsequential? Would they regard it as a tribute to their memory if our grief caused us to die while we were still living?

What if they could see that the influence of their lives inspired us to go forth to serve and bless the living? What if they could see that they had left upon our lives an afterglow of loving, and an echo in our hearts that blends in harmony with abiding love? Then their lives and our lives would not have been lost by dying.

READING OUR BOOK OF LIFE AND OUR OWN OBITUARY

Some of us inscribe the names of departed dear ones in a memorial book of life. What have their deaths inscribed upon our own book of life—misery, bitterness, and defeatism, or the determination to live more meaningfully and more lovingly for them and for ourselves?

Questions, questions, questions—all in search of answers, your answers.

We know what it means to make a living materially and economically. Do we know what it means to make a living spiritually and religiously? What is it that we really want out of life? A large income? Is this how to make a living? To be so concerned and so exclusively involved with money that we crowd everything else out of our minds? Are we so obsessed with the material that we say with P. T. Barnum of circus fame, "There's a sucker born every minute"? When he was dying, the last words Barnum ever uttered were, "What were today's receipts?" He died a rich man monetarily. His bank account was full, but was his heart empty of love, of tenderness, of compassion?

If we are really determined to make a living religiously and spiritually, then we have to ask ourselves, honestly and candidly, "If I were to die tomorrow, what would be my life's receipts? What has my life meant to me and to others?"

How do you think you would feel if you picked up an obituary column and read an account of your own death? This is what happened to Alfred Bernhard Nobel, nineteenth century Swedish chemist and engi-

neer, who developed and exploited the use of nitroglyc-
erin:

A relative with a similar name had died and a careless
journalist wrote an obituary for Alfred Nobel, of whom
he could say little more than that he was "a merchant
of death," and a master of destruction. Nobel was
greatly disturbed by the newspaper story of his life
which told of the fortunes he had amassed as a result of
his arming the nations of the world for war. It referred
to him as a cold-blooded and ruthless warmonger.

Then and there Nobel determined that the rest of his
days would be devoted to life's enrichment and the
betterment of humanity. To this task the Nobel fortune
was dedicated. He established the international Nobel
Peace Prize, and other Nobel Prizes for contributions
to literature, art, science, and medicine.

This raises the question: How many of us would
change for the better if we could read a critical obituary
of our own lives? Would we not think about what our
name has meant to others? Would we not resolve to
enrich the lives of others with some modest service to
our fellow human beings?

Actually, each of us does write his or her own obituary. The true biography of a person is the record of his
or her deeds; we write every word and every line of it.
If you were to write your own obituary, what would it
say? Vital statistics? Your vocation? The organizations
to which you belonged? Is that all? Is that all that can
be used to assess the worth of a human life?

No, your greatest accomplishments will never be
written in an obituary because they will never be recorded—your dedication to your family; your contributions to the welfare of others; the character and

strength you manifested in triumphing over grief, failure, and sorrow; and the fact that the world is a better
world because you have lived. This is what it means to
make a living, and this is the true measure of your life.

Dr. Viktor E. Frankl tells us that the world is not, as
an existentialist philosopher has seen it, a manuscript
written in a code we have to decipher. It is rather a
record which we have to dictate ourselves.

What are you and I dictating into that book of life
every moment, every hour, and every day? That we
have died while we are still living? That our hopes and
dreams of tomorrow have all died with us and await a
long-delayed burial? Or that we have refused to capitu-
late to despair and that we are daring to go on "beyond
the ragged edge of fortitude" to something more,
something promising, something that allows our grief
to send us forth to serve and bless the living?

WHY, MAN, WHY?

In a biblical commentary we are told that when
Moses and Aaron were mourning the death of their
sister Miriam, they sat in their tents and wept. Outside
the people were crying out because there was no water
for them or for their animals. Immersed in their grief,
the brothers were impervious to the pleas of the people
until they heard a heavenly voice command, "Hasten
from this place. You mourn the death of your sister who
is at peace, while my children thirst?" In other words,
God was saying, "Get back into the world and serve and
bless the living." No matter how deep our grief or how
anguished our souls, bereavement does not free us from
the responsibilities we have to life and to the living.

There are so many who need us. There is so much we

can do to alleviate human misery. The anonymous poet
knew this when he wrote:

I walked today through the slums of life, down the dark
streets of wretchedness and of pain. I trod today where
few have trod and as I walked I challenged God.

I saw the sots in the barrooms. I saw the prostitutes in
the dance halls. I saw the thieves as they picked pock-
ets. I saw men and women devoid of life, living in
worlds of sin, and above the din I whispered:
"Why, God, why?"

I walked today down the lanes of hate, hearing the jeers
of bitter men, hearing the names as they cursed and
spat: "Dago," "Nigger," "Kike," "Jap." I saw the dejected men they stoned. I felt the anguish of their cries.
I saw them as they slapped the lonely, as they turned
their backs on human needs. Snarling, growling were
the fiends of hell. These, God called His sons! Gasping
for air, I cried: "Why, God, why?"

I walked today through war's grim dregs—over fields of
blood, over graveless men. I saw the dead, the crucified,
the headless, the limbless, the pleading, the crying. I
saw the pain, the waste. I smelled the odor of rotted
flesh.

I saw the children gathered round—watching, naked,
hungry, weeping, diseased, dirty—the baby trying to
nurse from a dead mother. The ruins—the agony—the
despair! Disaster—disaster all around!

Blinded with tears, I fled down these streets. I stum-
bled, then stopped.

I shouted:

"Why, God, why? Why do you let man sin, hate, suffer?
"Unmerciful Father! God, art Thou blind? Art Thou
wicked and cruel? God, canst Thou watch and do
naught? Why must this be?"

The world grew silent. I awaited reply. The silence was
heavy. I started to tremble. I waited long, half rebuking,

half fearing. Then I heard from close behind me:
"Why, Man, why?"
Why, Man, why?

We write our own book of life, and it is always incomplete—there are blank pages for the future. We may be dissatisfied with what is written in our book of life now; we might like to erase lines and tear out pages. We know we cannot do that. But we can add acts of goodness, concern, caring, and loving kindness to the blank pages that still remain.

The years of life are all too brief. The days of love are short. We do not know how much time we have to add to the pages of our book of life. If we would honor the memory of our dead and allow death to serve the living, it is essential that we say with the anonymous poet,

I shall pass through this world but once.
Any good, therefore, that I can do, or any kindness
That I can show to any human being, let me do it now.
Let me not defer it or neglect it.
For I shall not pass this way again.

LIVING MEMORIALS

We place our offerings of bereavement on the altar of memory, but do we ever think that we may offer more than tears, anguished hearts, and sorrow as a memorial to those we love who are with us no more? What may we give them? What may we do for them?

An Indian maharajah had a beautiful and loving wife named Mahal. When she died, he felt that his soul had died too. One day an aged wise man said to him, "Oh, great Rajah, if you would keep the memory of your wife alive, build her a monument of jewels, marble, and

ivory, a monument that will make all men remember
Mahal, the beautiful."

The maharajah took the wise man's advice and built
a monument more beautiful than any other. Mahal's
memory was preserved forever in the exquisite beauty
of the Taj Mahal.

There are other memorials that are not adorned with
jewels, marble, or ivory. One such memorial is de-
scribed in an anecdote about Sir Christopher Wren, one
of the great architects of all time. Although he designed
fifty other churches and many public buildings, he is
most remembered for his masterpiece, St. Paul's Cathedral of London.

The old church was destroyed in the Great Fire of
London in 1666, and Sir Christopher was asked to restore it. He made many designs and models and finally
produced a cathedral whose beauty is unsurpassed.

Sir Christopher laid the foundation stone, and thirty-
five years later set the final stone in place. He rests
beneath the choir. The inscription on a tablet at the
north doorway is his epitaph: "Si monumentum requi-
ris, circumspice." ("Sir Christopher Wren. If you would
see his monument, look about you.")

Is it shocking to realize that you are a living memorial?

In a sense we are the living monuments, the living
memorials to our beloved dead. We are all the living
testimonials of their effect upon us. It may not be the
way we want it, but we attest to the influence and the
character impact of the years of their lives.

If this is so, we can understand why people are in-
creasingly turning away from expensive tombstones,
headstones, mausoleums, stone, marble, brass, and iron,
and instead creating memorials of service to the living.

I was initially intrigued with the concept of living

memorials about thirty-five years ago when I learned about two boys who established a friendship that was destined to last beyond death. They were inseparable during their school years. After graduation, they shook hands and said goodbye. One boy came from a well-to-do family and would soon start his premedical training at the University of California. The parents of the other boy were poor, so he had to get a job and forsake his own dream of becoming a doctor.

World War II came. The premed student joined the Air Force. The other went to work in a vital war industry. One day, the flier's mother received a telegram informing her that her son's plane had been shot down. Her son was dead.

He was an only son. She grieved and mourned continually. Others tried to comfort her but failed. Finally, an idea began to turn in her mind, an idea of a living memorial to her son. She sat down and wrote the following letter to his boyhood friend:

Dear Joe, By now, you must have heard of Arthur's death in action. I remember you when you were playing together, and I remember how fond you were of each other. Now he is gone, living on only in the hearts of those who loved him.

But I have thought of a way in which he can live on in another sense, a broader, more unselfish sense. Like him, you wanted to be a doctor, to ease human pain and suffering. But your family needed your help, so you did the only thing you could do at that time. But now you are more free.

If you are still interested in becoming a physician, I want you to be one. I want you to take Arthur's place at the university. Nothing would make me happier than to pay your way, every bit of it, and thus do for Arthur's best friend what I had hoped to do for him. I have thought of it as a sort of living memorial to him, and I know it is what he would want. . . .

Most of us do not have the means to send a worthy person through medical school. We cannot endow universities with chairs of learning in memory of those we love. We cannot establish scholarships or donate library shelves. But we can do something. What would be more constructive than to perpetuate the memory of our beloved dead with service to humanity? Every act of kindness in behalf of some human being, every deed of service to those in need, every dollar contributed to a worthy cause in behalf of the poor, the sick, and the deprived, is a memorial to our departed, and one that moves, walks, breathes, and lives.

THIS TOO CAN BE FOR GOOD

I used to hear an ancient adage from my parents and grandparents. Whenever anything tragic happened, they would repeat the Hebrew words, "Gam zu l'tovah," which means "This too is for the best." In time, I rebelled against this adage. If a child is born blind, how can you say "This too is for the best"? When there are floods, tornadoes, earthquakes, can we say "This too is for the best"? When there is genocide, a holocaust, when millions of people are brutally put to death, to say "This too is for the best" sounds cruel, irrational, and even blasphemous.

I thought this over and decided to examine the Hebrew phrase more carefully. A new meaning almost leaped up at me. The words really didn't say "This too is for the best." They really meant "This too can be for good." What a tremendous difference! I could believe and accept this. Even from tragedy, sorrow, and death,

some good can come if we make it so. Out of the unspeakable horror of the Nazi holocaust came a new
impetus for the establishment of the State of Israel. Out
of despotism arose a new concept of the democratic
process. Out of the ills and suffering of mankind came
the motivation for scientific and medical progress. Isn't
it possible that out of the human understanding which
emerges from bereavement great good mav come? So
much good done for humanity is the fruit of the efforts
of those who have taken their sorrows and transmuted
them into blessings of love, light, healing, and strength
for others. They have done it, and we can do it, too.

> Sir William Osler worked in the military hospitals of
> Britain during World War I. One day he was called out
> of the wards during his daily rounds to be given the
> word that his son had been killed on the fields of
> France. Stunned by this news, he still went back to pick
> up his rounds.
> For days the cheerful note was gone from his voice
> and associates no longer heard the tune which he often
> had whistled as he went from ward to ward. Though
> these never returned, something new came to take
> their place. A new compassion had come into his care
> of the soldiers who each day streamed in from the bat-
> tlefields. Before, he had had the professional concern of
> the physician so important to the practice of medicine;
> now there was added that discernible note of a personal
> compassion like that of a father for his son.

William Osler allowed death to serve the living and
so can we.

No one should say to you, no matter how kindly or
well-intentioned, that "this too is for the best" when a
dear one has died. If we say to ourselves, "This too can
be for good," we can validate their hopes and prayers

only by our actions. Death can be made for good when it inspires us to celebrate the blessings of life and death. "This too can be for good" may be said of both life and death.

A NEW DAWN AND A NEW LIGHT

For those of us who grieve, it has been such a long and painful night. The darkness seems to continue forever. Will we ever see a new dawn? Will morning ever come?

Alfred Tennyson must have pondered the same questions when he wrote about a lance made from wood that was "storm strengthened on a windy height." It came from a tree unshielded from the storms. The fierce winds hurled their fury against its roots and boughs, but to no avail—the winds and the storms only brought forth the latent stamina, power, and strength of the tree.

We, too, have withstood the power of the storms of grief and bereavement, and we have found a quality of strength that had been stored deep within our hearts. Grief entered our lives uninvited and unwelcome, but we are emerging from the storms and the darkness with a new faith and a sense of the beginning. We are beginning to hear the still, small voice of divinity even in the din of the storm and the clamor of the whirlwind. God speaks to us in storms even as birds sing to us in the darkness.

Will we allow the blow to destroy us, or will we permit the blow to radiate sparks and allow those sparks to shower upon us as reminders that the light has not been extinguished from our world or from our hearts? Will we see the sparks as a portent of the possibilities of a new dawn, a new light, and a new tomorrow?

Three sages were debating the question of when the night ends and the day begins. The first sage said, "The night ends, there is no longer darkness and a new day has begun when you can tell the difference between a blue thread and a green thread."

The second sage said, "The night ends and a new day begins when you can distinguish between a dog and a wolf."

The third sage said, "You are both wrong. The night ends, and there is no longer darkness, but the dawn of a new day comes when you can see the face of your brother."

When will the night of sorrow end? When will there be dawn, a new day, and a new beginning? When we are able to go beyond ourselves and see the faces of our brother and sister, those in our family, and those out there who need us.

We have confronted our grief, and now with renewed hope we find a source of power within that will enable us to go beyond ourselves, to make a covenant of compassion and concern with life. We may then make an amazing and wondrous discovery—we may discover a more meaningful, actualized, and fulfilled self when we are able to see the faces of our brothers and sisters. Then we will be able to see ourselves in them. When this happens, we will know that the long night of suffering has merged into a journey towards the dawn. We will know that morning has come as we behold the first rays of a new light and a new beginning.

Tomorrow is now. It is here. It is waiting for us.

One Step at a Time!

Make a list of ways you can make death serve the living.

۶۶ ۶۶

You write your own book of life. It is not too late to fill in blank pages through acts of kindness and concern. Take some action now!

۶۶ ۶۶

Think about some kind of a reasonable, practical living memorial. Do a deed of helpfulness to someone in need and do it in the name of your departed.

۶۶ ۶۶

Take the leap and the risk. Say to yourself, "I am ready now." The time for being a sad and passive observer is over. The time for being an active participant is now.

10
Your Greatest Hidden
Resource—You!

... and God created man in his own image ...
male and female created He them.
—Genesis 1:27

IT IS WRITTEN IN AN ancient manuscript, "After
Adam and Eve were expelled from Eden, God
caused a deep sleep to come over them. He then called
a council of angels and said to His heavenly hosts,
'When Adam and Eve awaken, they will know that they
are no longer divine, and they will go in search of their
divinity. Tell me, Angels, where shall I hide this Divinity?'

"One of the angels spoke and said, 'Lord of the Universe, let us conceal their Divinity within themselves,
for that is the last place they will go in search of it.'"

Do you agree that there is potential within you that
is a hidden resource for comfort and fulfillment? If you
do, you can reach within to find that great source of
strength. You have the power to manage your own life.
You have options to choose from. You have the auton-
omy to rule over your emotions and to determine your
present and your future.

Theologians tell us about a leap of faith. With competence and performance, you have the strength and the power within that will enable you to take a leap of action beyond grief and self-pity, beyond the inertia of bereavement and the helplessness of passivity.

Every human being is created in the spiritual image of God. The light and power of divinity shine and radiate within you. The mystic music of eternity vibrates and flows through you. The light is there, waiting to be seen. The power is waiting to be used. The music is waiting to be heard.

Your greatest hidden resource is within you. It can be found. It can be educed and used to help work through and beyond your grief, but only if you choose it.

I'VE TRIED, BUT . . .

As you read this you may be thinking, "This sounds reassuring, but I've tried so many times to find this source of strength within myself, and I've failed. I have really tried, but it doesn't work for me."

A friend of mine, a professor of English literature and a gifted poetic writer, lost his only child. He became embittered, hostile, and hopeless. I once asked him to turn to God and to pray with me. I do not remember his exact words, but this is the essence of what he said:

> You want me to pray? I've tried it and it doesn't work. When I pray, I want action and response. Prayer is okay for the mystic who can commune in some sort of metaphysical ecstasy with some sort of Supreme Being, but what about a man like me? Can prayer put together the pieces of my broken heart?
>
> You talk about God entering into our lives. Is there any way that God can enter a life that is black with despair, where darkness fills the void where a soul

should be? Can all the prayers in the world bring back the loving, living touch of my child now moldering and rotting in the grave, a companion to worms, cradled in everlasting nothingness?

"Pray to God" you said—commune with the Most High? I lift up my voice and shout until I'm hoarse. I croak froglike sounds and preface them with a proper "O Lord." I say, "My Heavenly Father, if You are my Father and I'm Your child, then it's Your child speaking. Hear me. Please! Hear me!"

I've tried it. I've begged God to enter my life, or just speak to me and give me some reason, some meaning for my loss. I've cried out, "God, if You don't want to speak with a voice, then just whisper, whistle, curse me, even *damn* me, but let me know that You are there, that something is there, that I'm not crying, pleading, and praying into an empty, unanswering nothingness." Do you know what happened? Nothing! I heard nothing. I felt nothing. And I'm supposed to believe that this inarticulate nothingness is an answer?

I look up and dust falls in my eyes. There is a spark within me, you say? I breathe upon it with hope. I fan it with wind, will, spirit, and all it does is fade out, winking obscenely as it dies. "Whatever Your name, God,—Lord, Jehovah, Allah, Zeus, Osiris, X,—look at me, I'm bowing, genuflecting, kneeling, prostrating myself. Let me see her and love her again, but if You can't bring back my darling, my beloved child, then help me to find a way to ease the torment and pain of my bereavement." If something, anything happens within me, then maybe there is a God and a God who responds to prayer.

Such a man cries out of the depths of his grief, and our hearts go out to him in his suffering. But the efficacy of prayer is not to be assessed by the poignancy of his suffering, the bitterness of his spirit, or the appeal to a God of magic to effect miraculous cures. It is understandable that he would feel more assured of the presence of God were he to hear a divine voice or even a heavenly whisper. However, the mature faith does not project a concept of God who articulates sounds.

Prayer cannot make us hear even a whisper spoken by God. Prayer will not ease the pain of a throbbing toothache, because prayer is not an equivalent of Novocain. Prayer will not cure cancer or arthritis. Prayer is not a resurrecting force that can bring back loved ones from the dead. But prayer can help us enter into communion with God.

GOD IS NEAR

A mature faith assures us not only that God *is,* but that God is *near, available,* and *accessible* to those who call upon Him in sincerity and in truth. In the words of Josiah Royce, "Through faith and prayer an individual may discover a Reality that enables one to face anything that can happen to one in the universe."

In eighteenth century Eastern Europe, the saintly Levi Yitzhak of Berditchev, called "The Compassionate," once lifted his voice to God at a time when the Jews were besieged by enemies. Heavily laden with sorrow, he cried out,

> Lord of the Universe, I do not beg You to reveal to me the secret of Your ways, for who am I to know them? But show me one thing, show it to me more clearly and more deeply, show me what this which is happening at this very moment means to me, what it demands of me, what You, Lord of the world, are telling me by way of it. Dear God, I do not ask You to take away my suffering;

I don't even want to know why I suffer; but only this, my God—do I suffer for Your sake?

The magnificence of such words reveals the true and basic meaning of prayer. The religious leader did not ask God to remove his suffering. He did not make of God a divine magician. All he wanted to know was whether his suffering was meaningful, whether his pain and misery were fulfilling some meaningful purpose.

Prayer does not change things. Prayer changes us and we change things. We cannot change God, but God can change us, if we seek and find the God within. We want God to hear our prayers, but it is more important that *we* hear our prayers, prayers that can lift us up out of the depths of sorrow to new plateaus and peaks of hope.

It is easy enough to have faith in God during periods of happiness, prosperity, and joy, when we are blessed with health and comfort. The test of faith is during those periods of suffering and pain, when the poison of doubt embitters our hope, when it seems that there is no possibility of personal happiness. To believe in God even when He seems to be silent, to love God when our lives, hopes, and dreams are placed in the crucible of anguish—this is the real test of faith.

DRIFTING OR STEERING, WHICH?

Sometimes we clothe our self-pity in garments of futility. We believe that whatever happens is the fault of others and that we have no choices or options, no share in the management of our lives. We are clay pigeons waiting to be shot down. We have been pushed into solitary confinement to eat the bread of affliction and drink the bitterness of our tears. We are orphans of the storms of continuous stress, coerced and compelled by a heartless, mindless, ruthless, and godless destiny.

If we continue to feel and think this way, then we are truly prisoners, victims, and losers, indentured to self-pity. How can God help us when we make no effort to help ourselves by utilizing our hidden resources?

There is no reward to this negative way of thinking. Could it be that consciously or subconsciously we want it to be this way so we will have a good excuse to continue to ask, "Why me? Why, God, why?"

Nobody can know the extent of your heartache. Nobody can know how often, how hard, and how much you have tried. You may think, "Everybody wants me to take charge of my grief and my life. How can I?" The question is: Are you going to continue to take refuge in a sanctuary of tears, or are you going to exercise the power of choice?

YOU HAVE THE POWER TO CHOOSE

Many self-help books correctly insist that each of us has the power of choice, and this is relatively true. There are some circumstances over which we have no choice. There are others over which we do.

You choose the way you want to be. If you are helpless, lonely, and defeated, you have chosen this for yourself. It is true you have not chosen the causes of your grief, but you have chosen the way you are coping with your grief. "I can't" are perhaps the most lying and inaccurate words in the human vocabulary. Most of us *can* if we want to. Our objective is to *want to.*

We have the power to say, "I don't choose to continue on this way. I am a person with the right to choose and I will choose life, and the beckoning possibilities of a new tomorrow. There isn't anyone or anything that can keep me down but me. And I won't allow it to happen or continue any longer."

If you have chosen to go on grieving forever, if you have chosen to refuse to seek the zest of life, if that is the way you want it, you have made your choice, so you might as well accept it without complaining and self-pity. You have given up your sovereignty as a person. You have chosen passivity, inertia, and defeatism. You are the one who surrendered. You are the one who quit on life. Admit it—you did not choose your loss and bereavement, but you did choose to let it control and conquer you.

Is there anything you can do about this? Yes, there is. You can start by thinking of yourself more positively and optimistically.

Just Who Do You Think You Are?

Men and women are creative beings with freedom of will, with a potential for truth, justice, compassion and loving. Would you rather believe this or believe with Jean Paul Sartre, the high priest of the existentialists, that "Man is the incommensurable idiot of the universe," or with Bertrand Russell, who claimed that "Man, with his knowledge of good and evil, is but a helpless atom," or with H. L. Mencken, who taught that "Man is a sick fly, taking a dizzy ride on a gigantic fly-wheel"?

If man is "the incommensurable idiot of the universe," let him squirm and struggle in the straitjacket of his own maniacal misery. He belongs in it. If man, "with his knowledge of good and evil, is but a helpless atom," let him dangle, a cosmic orphan in a parentless universe, without freedom of will to act, to love, to create a moral society. For if there is no morality, there is no purpose. There are only the winds of chance that drive and blow him through a meaningless mockery of time. If man is a "sick fly," then swat him, crush him, smash him as you would any other such filthy disease-carrying insect.

If man is a robot, a thing, a mass occupying space, a machine conditioned by his environment, determined by his genes and compelled by his animal drives, then there is not much choice. If we believe this, then freedom of will is a myth and our lives are dictated by a mechanical determinism that permits no options.

If, however, we think of man struggling and groping to emerge from the jungle into a better tomorrow, endowed with freedom of will and a divine potential for beauty, truth, holiness, and loving, then we can begin to find a new respect, not only for mankind, but for ourselves.

ACT THE WAY YOU WANT TO FEEL

How do you begin the search within for your greatest potential? Begin by acting the way you want to feel, and it will help you to feel the way you act!

A minister friend of ours was once asked how he could go directly from a funeral to a wedding without allowing his sadness to show. He told us, "What else can I do? Even though I grieve and mourn with the family, I can't bring sorrow to the happiness of young people and their families on their sacred day. So I go through a psychological masquerade. Even though I don't feel like it, when I leave the mortuary, I smile, I whistle, and I hum. I think of happy experiences and concentrate on what a wonderful day this is for the young people, and, you know, after a while, even though it's only an act, I do feel better and I'm able to carry on."

We can do the same thing. Yes, it is extremely difficult to begin. It is almost impossible for us to force ourselves out of our grieving mood, but we can do it, if we try hard enough. The important thing is to begin to make the effort to put on a smiling face and to act. So what if, at the beginning, it is phony? We have often smiled when we have not felt like it. We can do it again.

Do not take failure for a final answer. Try feeling better, and when it does not work keep on trying and keep on acting. You may discover that you are starting to feel the way you are acting.

There are spiritual resources within us that we have not even started to tap. It is possible, it is feasible, and it is real to utilize the spiritual power within.

We are all familiar with the term "psychosomatic," the influence of the mind upon the body. We have heard of faith healing and spiritual healing. If the mind can influence the body, the mind can also influence our feelings, making us glad or sad, sick or well. We all know that when we think sad, we feel sad. The same thing can happen when we think happy.

We have witnessed incredible changes in our bodies when we have been nervous, anxious, and frightened. That is because a gland called the hypothalamus together with the pituitary and the autonomic-sympathetic-nervous system sends chemical and hormonal messages to our bodies through our brains. When we are uneasy and frightened our lips and mouths become dry, we perspire, and we feel the need to go to the bathroom. We have butterflies in our stomachs; our heartbeat accelerates; our blood pressure elevates; and we feel ourselves flushed and uptight. What happens when fear and anxious thoughts are gone? Through a process called homeostasis, or glandular hormonal balance, our bodies readjust and we feel better.

This process can apply to our grief thoughts and feelings, too. Through prayer, positive thinking, faith, will, and action, we have the power to regulate and influence our thoughts and feelings in order to deal with our sorrow and bereavement.

This is not some kind of religious magic. "Psychological" comes from the word "psyche" which means soul. "Psychology" then means the "study of the soul." Psychosomatic can in turn mean the influence of the soul upon the body. Our hidden resources can help us to regulate our own spiritual thermostats in order to bring about a balance in our thoughts and feelings so that we can start to live again.

ONLY ONE MILE TO MAKE

The effort to delve within ourselves to find and utilize our greatest potential may seem to be too overwhelming to accomplish. When we think this way, we should remember a lesson veteran newsman Eric Sevareid once learned:

> When he was seventeen years old, Sevareid and a school pal set out to travel by canoe from Minneapolis to the historic fur trading post of York Factory on Hudson Bay.
>
> The last leg of the journey was the most difficult and dangerous. Stretched before them were 450 miles of rugged wilderness with only one permanent settlement in the entire distance. The boys were awed by the prospect.
>
> Just as they were about to set out, an old fur trader gave them this advice: "Just think about the next mile you have to go, not about the ones after that, never about 450."
>
> Sevareid says that this advice stayed with him through the years. "Many times in the future," he re-

calls, "I was to rediscover that there is only one mile to make, never 450."

The long journey through mourning is made only one step at a time, and then one mile at a time. We can live in the same way, so that we travel one step at a time, one day at a time, one problem at a time, never 450 at a time.

As you make the effort to find and use your greatest hidden potential, be gentle with yourself and keep your expectations reasonable. You can and will succeed. The source of strength is there. You have to go in search of it.

OTHERS HAVE DONE IT AND SO CAN YOU

Failure, frustration, despair, guilt, and grief are a part of life. There is not one of us who can live without experiencing physical, emotional, and mental pain.

Hans Selye, the noted scientist and physician, believes that the only way we can avoid the stresses of life is through death and dreamless sleep. He is right. Without some kind of stress we would be without motivation. Without the challenges and uncertainties of life we would be devoid of excitement and creativity. Furthermore, we would never learn to use the human and divine potential that God has given to us; we would have no reason to seek and find the hidden resources within.

When we draw a bow against the loose strings of a violin there is no music. It is only when the strings of a violin are taut, bound tightly, and under stress that we are able to make music.

So it is with us. It is only when we are under stress

that we are able to make the music within us. It is only when we are bound to sorrow and despair that we are able to find the freedom and the will to transcend our anguish by making the music of the human spirit. We never really see the stars in the sky until the earth's light goes out. We never see the beauty of a rainbow without the storm cloud.

When it seems that you can never put the stars back into your sky and that sorrow has made you deaf to the music of life, be assured that you have the power to rely on your hidden resources within. Others have done it, so can you.

TEARS INTO DREAMS

Jacob slept with stones as a pillow and dreamed of a ladder rising to heaven. He converted his sorrow into a vision of supernal holiness. He found the inner resources to behold God, even through his tears.

Moses found God in darkness. The prophets heard the still small voice of divinity even amidst the clamor of mocking voices and physical suffering.

The Psalmists offered us an enduring legacy of spiritual strength. The Psalms grew out of the pain of men who cried, "Out of the depths do I call unto Thee, O Lord. God, hearken unto my voice; let Thine ears be attentive to the voice of my supplications. . . . O Lord, hear my prayer, and let my cry come unto Thee. Hide, not Thy face from me in the days of my despair." Despite their anguish, these men found hidden resources of the spirit to sustain them and guide them into the light—and so can we.

Have you ever heard Beethoven's Ninth Symphony? Beethoven was tormented by disease, struggling through titanic inner conflict. His soul hungered to hear the music he was composing. His very being clamored to comprehend the stirring chords emerging from the depths of his creative genius. But he could not hear his own music because Beethoven was deaf.

"Paradise Regained," one of the most majestic of all poems, emerged from Milton's blindness. Lord Byron, the man with the club foot, the man with the agonized soul, wrote magnificent poetry. Robert Louis Stevenson, wracked with tuberculosis, hardly able to breathe, converted his pain and tears into sublime literature. Florence Nightingale and Helen Keller served and blessed others despite their pain and suffering.

Like the Biblical Job, Steinmetz the scientist, Pascal the philosopher, Louis Pasteur, Thomas Edison, Elizabeth Barrett Browning, Sigmund Freud, and Cole Porter surmounted physical and emotional pain when they found the hidden resources to enable them to make their contributions to science, literature, and music.

Throughout human history, men and woman of all faiths have converted their tears into dreams, even though they had to rest their heads on pillows of adversity. The victims of the Nazi holocaust knew that their cups of misery had been filled to overflowing. The tears of suffering that once trickled into those cups grew into a hot, steady stream, each drop distilled from the bitter cruelty and anguish of a suffering humanity. The tears poured over the rim and became a raging torrent, a boiling deluge leaping up to the roaring of a million claps of thunder, scalding a world in which such things can be. But somehow those who suffered heard the still small voice. Despite their suffering, they made their contributions to medicine, art, literature, and the sciences. But more important, heroic men and women of all faiths gave testimony to the strength and power of a human spirit that could not be vanquished.

Elie Wiesel, the poet of the Holocaust, should be a bitter man. He saw his own family murdered. He witnessed the torture of his friends and neighbors for years. And yet he writes poetry about dust turned to hope, about keeping alive the promise of tomorrow, about building a better world for all of God's children everywhere. He was able to find the spiritual resources within to enable him to go on, and so can we.

YOUR GREATEST RESOURCE

When the students of Zusya approached their dying teacher, he whispered to them, "Oh, my students, I'm so afraid!"

Shocked, they responded, "Our teacher, have you not always taught us that we should have no fear of dying because God is our Father—a God filled with compassion and loving kindness?"

"That is true," Zusya replied, "but that is not why I am afraid. I'm not afraid that when I stand before the Throne of Judgment God will say to me, 'Zusya, why were you not a Moses?' because I am not Moses. And I am not afraid God will say to me, 'Why were you not an Isaiah?' because I am not Isaiah. But, my students, I'm afraid, terribly afraid that when God will ask me, 'Zusya, why were you not Zusya? Why didn't you live up to the best that Zusya could have been?' What shall I answer?"

That applied to Zusya. What about us? Have we lived up to the best we could have been? Have we reached for the highest in our human potential?

You have tremendous power within you. You can take charge of your own life. You can shift gears. You can change. You can choose to endure the night of mourning and behold the dawn of a new morning. You can choose because there is God power, and that God power is within you.

"And God said, 'When Adam and Eve awaken, they will know that they are no longer divine, and they will go in search of their divinity. Tell me, Angels, where shall I hide this divinity?'

"One of the angels spoke and said, 'Lord of the Universe, let us conceal their divinity within themselves, for that is the last place they will go in search of it.' "

One Step at a Time!

Consider the reality that you are created in the spiritual image of God.

ఆక్ష ফ৯

Think about the ways you express your grief and ask yourself what these grief expressions are doing to you and to others.

ఆక్ష ফ৯

Make a choice to take charge of your life.

ఆక్ష ফ৯

Act the way you want to feel and it will help you to feel the way you are acting.

ఆక్ష ফ৯

Keep your expectations reasonable and think about the next step and the next day—not your entire future.

ఆక్ష ফ৯

Turn your tears into dreams. Others have done it and so can you.

ఆక్ష ফ৯

Search for and use the God-power within yourself. Accept the belief that your greatest hidden resource is you.

Now Is the Time for the
Biggest Step of All

You must move forward to renewed life and live again. Now is the time to restructure your life, to smile again, to laugh again, to love again. Now is the time to taste the flavor of excitement and feel a growing eagerness for the zest of new adventure, to experience the anticipatory excitement of winning and losing. Now is the time to reopen old doors and to open new doors to the promise of joyous fulfillment.

Make yourself ready to step forth into the struggles, challenges, and the celebration of life—now!

You have the will power and the God-power to make this happen. You can do it! Millions of others have done it, and so can you!

When it does happen, and you return to the world of the living, it will not be the ending of mourning, but a new dawn and a new beginning for you and for those you love. Then will the memory of your dear departed truly be for blessing.

ABOUT THE AUTHORS

William B. Silverman has served as congregational rabbi in pulpits across the United States and is author of a number of books, including *The Sages Speak: Rabbinic Wisdom and Jewish Values*. Kenneth M. Cinnamon, Ph.D., is a clinical psychologist, author, and consultant.